D0099212

WITHDRAWN

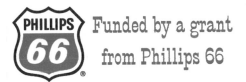

Funded by a grant
from Phillips 66

Also by Gabrielle Glaser

The Nose: A Profile of Sex, Beauty, and Survival
Strangers to the Tribe: Portraits of Interfaith Marriage

Her Best-Kept Secret

WHY WOMEN DRINK—AND
HOW THEY CAN REGAIN CONTROL

GABRIELLE GLASER

Simon & Schuster
New York London Toronto Sydney New Delhi

Simon & Schuster
1230 Avenue of the Americas
New York, NY 10020

First Simon & Schuster hardcover edition July 2013

SIMON & SCHUSTER and colophon are registered trademarks of Simon & Schuster, Inc.

For information about special discounts for bulk purchases, please contact Simon & Schuster Special Sales at 1-866-506-1949 or business@simonandschuster.com.

The Simon & Schuster Speakers Bureau can bring authors to your live event. For more information or to book an event contact the Simon & Schuster Speakers Bureau at 1-866-248-3049 or visit our website at www.simonspeakers.com.

Permissions for photographs appear on page 229.

Designed by Aline C. Pace

Manufactured in the United States of America

10 9 8 7 6 5 4

Library of Congress Cataloging-in-Publication Data

Glaser, Gabrielle.
    Her best-kept secret : why women drink—and how they can regain control / Gabrielle Glaser. — First Simon & Schuster hardcover edition.
        pages cm
    Includes bibliographical references.
1. Women—Alcohol use—United States. 2. Women alcoholics—Rehabilitation—United States. I. Title.
    HV5137.G56 2013
    362.292082'0973—dc23

                                                      2013001088

ISBN 978-1-4391-8438-7
ISBN 978-1-4391-8440-0 (ebook)

In memory of Nana and Poppy,
wholly immoderate in courage, affection, and fun

Contents

Her
Best-Kept
Secret

Prologue

My name is Gabrielle, and I'm not an alcoholic.

In the field of women who write about alcohol, that makes me unusual. Much of the memorable writing on this subject comes from women who have suffered from their abuse of alcohol—with broken marriages, ugly custody battles, and repeated DUIs. These addiction chronicles trace the now-familiar path from debauchery to redemption with lively anecdotes about waking up in the beds of men whose names the author can't or doesn't want to remember.

This is not one of those books.

I'm a journalist who has written about the overlapping universes of women, health, and culture for two decades. A few years ago, I started noticing signs that women were drinking more—a lot more. I saw it in the consumption of young women who seemed determined to keep up with the boys and continued on through the stumbles of early adulthood. Women well into the responsible years of family and career were boozing it up—my friends; my neighbors; even, on occasion, me.

As I began to explore the overlapping universes of women and alcohol, I wanted to understand what I was noticing all around me: from glossy ads to my own refrigerator; from social networking to television. I have lived in a lot of places, moving from the East to the West and back again, and the trend was evident wherever I looked.

When my oldest daughter entered kindergarten in the mid-1990s, wine wasn't a part of obligatory school functions in the New York suburbs where I lived with my family. But a few years later, when my second daughter entered school, a couple of mothers joked about bringing their flasks to Pasta Night. *Flasks?* I wondered, at the time. Wasn't that, like, from *Gunsmoke?*

In 2001, I had a third child, and even without looking hard I could see that something had significantly shifted. It was a few months after 9/11, and loving friends dropped off dinner, flowers, and baby clothes. Everybody seemed happy for a break in the terrible news. (Nine people in my small town had been killed in the towers.) But several women—editors, advertising executives, marketing consultants—delivered unusual presents. I got wine—lots of it—in binary wine carriers that reminded me of double strollers. "You'll be needing this!" was the general message. Two people told me: "One for you, one to share." It was an anxious time, but even so it struck me as odd. Why would I drink a bottle of wine by myself? I was nursing, for God's sake. I chalked it up to my surroundings, where, in the middle of memorial services and anthrax scares, stress was at a peak. If you weren't drinking at that time, you had to have a pretty damn good excuse. Still, wine as a baby gift?

In 2002, my husband and I got jobs at a newspaper in Oregon, where I have roots stretching back 150 years. Almost as soon as we were settled in Portland, I noticed women even in that relaxed city bending their elbows with the same enthusiasm as stressed-out New Yorkers. It was against company rules to drink on the job, but women I interviewed routinely paired their lunches with beers and wine flights. After work, I occasionally joined some female colleagues who met at a cozy wood-paneled bar across the street. They were regulars, and the bartenders usually had their drinks poured the minute they took off their coats. I always left after one glass of wine—my kids were young, and I wanted to get home to make dinner. My coworkers stayed, usually for another couple of rounds, then drove home on the rainy roads. It wasn't as if I was sipping herbal tea at night myself: I usually had a small juice glass of wine while I was cooking, and another small one during dinner. But evenings at the bar used to make me a little worried. Those women sort of . . . tied one on. What if someone got into an accident, and I hadn't said anything?

I realized that it wasn't just the pressure of meeting deadlines. Women drank if they worked; women drank if they didn't work. They even drank at the parent meetings for the laid-back environmental middle school. There was no need for flasks there—half the time, gatherings were in wine bars.

Women drank in my sister's elegant suburb, before dinner, during dinner, instead of dinner. They drank just as much in my hipster neighborhood on the other side of the river, too. One Sunday night as I was doing the dishes, I saw a woman with an ancient yellow Lab pause on the parking strip outside next to the recycling bin, out for the next morning's pickup. She glanced around furtively, then shifted her backpack around to her chest. She slid first one giant empty green bottle into the plastic box, and then another. She did this as noiselessly as one might move a sleeping baby from the car seat to the crib, so as not to disturb. At first I thought maybe she had just forgotten to take out her own bin, but those big merlot bottles were there every Monday morning for the next six years.

It became clear that this wasn't just in New York and Portland. My survey was decidedly unscientific, but wide ranging. Women drank in Seattle, they drank in Chicago, they drank in San Francisco. They just . . . drank.

•　　•　　•

As I began to think about this book, I realized that drink was more of a subtext in my own life than I had understood. As a child, it was a thrill for me to stride into rural Oregon bars and pool halls with my granddad, a handsome French Canadian with deep-set blue eyes, the nose of a hawk, and smooth broad cheekbones that looked like they'd been chiseled from marble. Poppy managed a jukebox and pinball-machine operation his brother-in-law owned, and when we would walk into a place—nobody cared much about minors not being allowed—people sat up and took notice. The bars made me feel like I was visiting Jeannie in her bottle. The wall, incandescent with green gin, topaz whiskey, and gleaming vodka, looked to me like a library of giant jewels. The cocktail waitresses always gave me Shirley Temples loaded with maraschino cherries, plastic monkeys dangling from the side of the tall glass.

Poppy had come to the United States as a teenager, in the midst of Prohibition, and his knowledge of the Canadian border's back roads came in handy during that long dry spell. Only after he died did I understand what he had meant when he joked that he had been in the "thirst" business.

My parents weren't teetotalers, but they were hardly big tipplers, either. Drinks were for special occasions: my dad liked Black Russians, but only in restaurants, and once on vacation my mom ordered a Blue Hawaii. When I was in high school in the early 1980s, somebody would pass around a bottle of MD 20/20, or draw a crowd with a case of contraband Rainier someone had begged an older brother to buy. The beer was invariably warm, and invariably bad, and I could never understand what the fuss was about.

In college, I got really drunk a single time, on a bottle of Cracklin' Rose. It was the fall of 1982, and as freshmen we envisioned the need for some sort of terrific mass relief after our first set of midterms. We organized an evening with a purpose, something we called The Get Drunk and Fall Down Party. I drank most of my bottle and spent many hours that night trying to calm my spinning bed. I was eighteen and stupid, but I learned a fast lesson. For two years after, I worked hard and rarely drank.

But then I went to study in France. The girls who lived across the hall in my squat concrete dorm always kept their door open, Gallic insouciance on constant display. They sat cross-legged on the floor and smoked cigarettes, tapping away at their typewriters and occasionally pouring Bordeaux from the collection of half-drunk bottles on their desks. The boys had brown bottles of Kronenbourg 1664 in a small refrigerator in the hallway, and the students shared drinks like American students stuck their hands in bowls of air-popped popcorn. Not once did I hear the slurred squawks and boozy bellows so common on my campus six thousand miles away.

On weekends, I lived with a couple outside Paris who were friends of my parents. Guy, my host, made a delightful show of presenting his wife, Arlette, and me with beautiful pink Kirs, and he was even more theatrical about the wine he had chosen to accompany the meal. Usually we drank a bottle among the three of us; sometimes more. We did the same thing at Paris restaurants on Saturdays. They were never drunk, and neither was I. Moderation is easy if that's what everyone does.

Ever since, I have enjoyed wine most nights in pretty much the same way, except when I've been sick or pregnant. My husband and I drink wine with dinner, finish perhaps two-thirds of the bottle, and put it away for the next night. In the summer, or when we have guests, sometimes we drink cocktails.

But a few years ago, I began to notice distressing articles — "Moderate Drinking Poses Breast Cancer Risk" — or questionnaires in women's magazines asking "Are you an alcoholic?" No matter how low my score, I still felt the slightest bit unsettled: Was there something I was missing? Did I like drinking too much, look forward to it too much, enjoy what felt like a wintergreen Certs coat my veins about a half hour after I'd had my small glass? Did liking it mean I had some sort of a problem? Nonsense, I'd think: I don't get drunk, I never black out, I've never dreamed of hiding my consumption. And besides, the French and the Italians drink much, much more, more regularly, and they're not alcoholics. But wait, said the news crawl of worries that advances through my brain daily. What if they are? The logical counterargument responds: Don't be such a prig! Moderate drinkers outlive everybody, and even heavy drinkers outlive teetotalers. I almost never have more than two of those little glasses a night.

Except a few years ago, when I was leaving my job and extended family in Oregon. I was trying to find a house in suburban New Jersey over the Internet, sell one I'd hoped never to leave, and had frequent long-distance quarrels with my husband, who was commuting between Portland and his great new job in New York. My parents were sad. My sister and I snapped at each other. My teenagers were angry and tense; my youngest daughter, then six, was bewildered. Whenever I stopped to see my parents-in-law, who had moved from Boston to a retirement community near us, I felt an anvil of guilt.

And that is how, during a rainy Pacific Northwest winter, I found myself anticipating my nightly wine.

On my last day of work, I made sure I waited to cry until I got to my car with a box of my belongings: yellowed clippings, a vase, my photographs. I followed the Willamette River eastward, finally sobbing as I crossed my favorite red bridge. Mount Hood glowed pink in the eastern sky. I drove past my quirky gym, which was also a video store that carried independent films; past a guy on a unicycle; past the tapas bar we could walk to; past the giant old-growth fir trees. I could feel a headache, the kind I get from crying, crawling up my skull.

Until that moment, drinking to steady my nerves hadn't really ever occurred to me—and certainly not when I was by myself. I might feel a little looser after drinking, but I always stopped. I always hated the sensation of losing control.

That night (and several that followed), I found myself hating it a lot less than usual. Here is what I told myself: I knew the small juice glasses I used for wine held five ounces, because long ago I measured them, just like the posters on the back of my doctor's door advised. So that one-third of a bottle isn't actually your "one glass." My glasses were what American guidelines consider a "serving," and I never filled it to the top—only sots would do such a thing. So my ordinary two glasses weren't even two servings. Besides, I was supposed to drink a glass of red wine every night. My dad's cardiologist told me so himself, as my dad recovered from triple-bypass surgery. Okay, so I preferred white. It had to have some helpful effect, too.

I got home, pulled open the refrigerator, and opened my favorite wine, a sauvignon blanc from New Zealand. The girls were watching TV and didn't have much interest in talking to me anyway. I started cooking and dialed my husband in New York. I poured, drank, poured some more. The girls and I ate dinner, during which I poured some more. We cleaned up. I eyed the bottle on the counter, alarmed. It was two-thirds gone. And five days later, I realized I had polished off two other bottles. Alone.

One afternoon, after leaving my house several times so that unexpected prospective buyers might roam it freely, my heartbeat felt like a car alarm. I was on deadline with a free-lance magazine piece, but the day was spent. I looked anxiously at the clock. It was 4:45, too early to drink. I took the dog for a walk, and suddenly felt my face flush hot. What was I thinking? What about wine at five o'clock would make that day better? What was it about wine—too much of it, at least— that was making anything better?

So to test myself, I stopped for a couple of weeks. No drinking, no buying. In the grape-producing western states, the vegetable-museum supermarkets have aisles of wine, stacked high, with helpful aproned stewards there to pluck out just the right bottle to go with your salmon, your roast chicken, your barbecued lamb. Proud winery representatives stand behind makeshift bars with tiny plastic tasting cups, inquiring if you'd like to try some. *Why, thank you, I would.* Safeway gives out free cloth wine totes whenever you buy six bottles. You can even buy wine at the gas station, not that you would. But you could. It's everywhere. I hadn't even noticed—until I looked.

I passed my little test, but I also gained an understanding. I saw how easily, how swiftly, how imperceptibly you could slip into a habit. Since then, I keep a strict internal log: no more than two drinks on any night, a few nights a week with none. I can't say I feel better, or notice even the slightest difference on the nights I don't drink—or the mornings after.

Even so, this usually bumps my tally to more than seven drinks a week (though not by much), and by U.S. standards that makes me a "heavy drinker." This strikes me as odd, since the government guidelines for "safe" female drinking in Australia, Denmark, Canada, Holland, and New Zealand roughly double that of the United States. In the wine-producing countries of Italy, France, and Spain, recommendations for moderate daily limits are even higher.

In August 2008, just as the economy was tanking, my family and I moved to New Jersey. Everything looked pretty bleak, and again I noticed women joking about how much they were imbibing. When I stopped at a liquor store for some Spanish wine to pair with paella one hot day, my eye was drawn to the opposite side of the store, where women in microscopic miniskirts presided over a display of dry ice. They were promoting a new drink called "Sparkling Nuvo," a clear pink concoction made of vodka, sparkling white wine, and passion fruit juice. "It's like vodka and champagne!" said a young woman as she stroked her long hair. I was decidedly not the demographic they were after, and no one noticed when I took a whiff of the viscous stuff. It looked and smelled like Benadryl.

As I glanced down the rows of booze past the women, though, I recognized that I had missed a dramatic cultural shift. In the years I'd been in Oregon, I hadn't set foot in a liquor store because my alcohol of choice—wine—is sold on every corner there. In New Jersey, it's usually only available in specialty outlets. And much of the merchandise I saw was perched in what could only be described as the Lady Aisle. I wandered past complete mysteries: watermelon-flavored vodka, vanilla-flavored vodka (wouldn't that just be called vanilla?), even pink tequila. There were odd foil pouches of pre-mixed cocktails that boasted how they took the "guesswork" out of mixing drinks. Capri Sun for moms!

The week I saw the Sparkling Nuvo, I made a trip to my town's recycling depot. We had finally finished unpacking, and I wanted to get rid of the boxes I had shoved into the backseat of my car. Once I found the place, behind a high chain-link fence, I noticed a long line of luxury metallic SUVs with female drivers. One after the other, they parked next to the truck for metal and glass and jumped out of their seats. Like the merlot drinker in Portland, these women had a singular mission: to deposit their shameful proof and leave as quickly as possible. Expert multitaskers, these women did not speak on their iPhones—the violent crash of the bottles, crunching into the iron maws of the trucks, would have been a dead giveaway. Their arms, ropey from years of yoga or miles on the elliptical trainer—"Best shape of her life!"—reached for the bags that are the totems of upper-middle-class life: silver ones from Nordstrom, white ones from Williams-Sonoma, plain ones from Whole Foods. Out poured the bottles, the bottles, the bottles. The bottles they intend to start just sipping from, but end up finishing before their husbands get home.

"Here every week," said John, who mans the depot on Wednesdays. He folded his three middle fingers into his palm, and extended his pinkie and his thumb. He cocked his head back and pointed his thumb toward his open mouth, as if it were the neck of a bottle. He smiled, and shook his head.

On a sunny July Sunday in 2009, a thirty-six-year-old Long Island mother named Diane Schuler killed her daughter, her three nieces, herself, and three men in an oncoming car when she careened the wrong way up a New York highway.

At first, sympathy swirled around Schuler, who reminded women of themselves. She had juggled a marriage, two kids, and a job—in her case, as an executive at Cablevision. The Taconic Parkway, the road where she crashed, is notorious for accidents, and initial reports focused on the possibility that a medical condition had disoriented her. But when the toxicology report from her mangled body revealed that she had a blood alcohol level at twice the legal limit, as well as trace THC, the psychoactive ingredient in marijuana, compassion turned to contempt. "How Could She?" demanded the *New York Post*. Her widower insisted, even years later, that his wife couldn't have had a secret drinking problem—despite the fact that ten shots of vodka were in her bloodstream at death. "She was a great mother," he has said.

Great mothers, of course, can't have hidden drinking problems.

Women who drink face more scrutiny than men. But the most vitriol is reserved for mothers who drink too much.

Several weeks after the Taconic tragedy, news of a second accident, also caused by a drunken mother, blared across New York tabloids. This time, a Bronx woman, blitzed on cognac, flipped her carful of girls while speeding on the Henry Hudson Parkway. Eleven-year-old Leandra Rosado, a friend of her daughter's, died after she was thrown from the car, and outrage about the incident was so palpable that New York legislators swiftly made driving while drunk with a child in the car a felony. In the nine months that followed, police made 514 arrests under the new law. And while 63 percent of drunken drivers were men, it was the women who stirred the most outrage—and the most news coverage.

A handful of mug shots of the men appeared in local and metropolitan papers, but inebriated women invariably warranted bigger headlines: "Boozed-Up Mom Charged" and "Drunk Mom Behind Wheel." Online commenters dished predictable invective: "Disgusting excuse for a mother!" "Feed her to the wolves!" "Poor white trash!" They have been shamed, then forgotten. Written off. Barflies.

There is another realm of women drinkers—those who fear they drink too much but haven't yet suffered serious consequences. They don't intend to cross that line, but sometimes there are scary signs: drunken e-mails, wholly forgotten until morning; angry words blurted when the salve of wine morphs into a serum for ugly truths.

Online, in posts to perfect lady-strangers, the women confess. They unburden themselves to other worried drinkers who find that their own jobs and cooking and homework and college applications and clothes left in the dryer—for the love of *God*, can't somebody, anybody, please match the *socks* in this house?—are all a little easier to cope with after they pour themselves a nice glass of chardonnay, or zinfandel, but probably chardonnay. They have the sneaking suspicion that the one glass that slid into two and then three and, oh, what the hell, now four, is a bad sign.

They try many things. They try not buying alcohol. They try drinking only on weekends. They try drinking pomegranate juice with seltzer. They try putting ginger tea over ice. They try sucking Jolly Ranchers. They pick up the cigarettes they last smoked in college. They love, love, love the days they wake up clearheaded. They read at night, they watch TV at night, they are sometimes more, sometimes less, interested in sex. But then something happens: a snide comment at work; the check for camp that goes missing in the backpack vortex; a nasty driver in the supermarket parking lot. A trigger, one of the many that drip, drip, drip like water seeping from a leaky roof, and the cork comes off. The glass gets poured. Down the hatch.

But let's be clear: The trigger is usually quite simple. It is evening itself.

The worry festers. Do I have a problem? Am I some sort of lush?

* * *

Today's excess imbibing is only the latest sharp swing in America's complex relationship with alcohol. I wondered how, exactly, did our cultural icons go from the saloon destroyer Carry Nation to the Cosmopolitan-sipping Carrie Bradshaw in just a couple of generations? How had we gotten from abstinence crusades to Girls Gone Wild and, for women a few years older, furtive trips to the dump?

Over the two and a half years I spent talking to women for this book, I found only a few who were willing to reveal themselves. Some cited the writer Stefanie Wilder-Taylor, who had created an identity for herself as a drinking mom in such books as *Sippy Cups Are Not for Chardonnay*. In 2009, though, Wilder-Taylor, the mother of three young daughters, announced on her blog that she drank too much and needed some help stopping. She cofounded an online group for women struggling with alcohol, the Booze-Free Brigade, that has grown to fifteen hundred members.

Yet because female excess drinking is a shame to be hidden at all costs, the drinking stays hidden, revealing itself at jewelry parties where Heather or Denise stay a little too close to the wine, a little too far away from the earrings. In today's confessional world, where even e-vites seem to demand elaborate explanations for why guests can't make it to a birthday party, the women worry. In my small town, the wine store owners, like hairdressers, hear everything. One told me that she has a customer who always asks for the store's fancy gift bags, as if somehow sheathing the same bottles of cheap pinot grigio she buys will help repackage the truth. Another woman comes in once a week to get several liters of inexpensive cabernet—"for cooking," she says, as she races to the back of the store, then plunks down exact change. "Must be making a lot of coq au vin," the store owner says.

American women afflicted with some form of embarrassing excess or painful deficiency have a lot of modern help. If you have an "overactive bladder," there are a handful of drugs about which you may "ask your doctor," and if you're depressed, you might take anything from Abilify to Zoloft. There are whole industries of fat-busters: appetite suppressants, fat-absorption inhibitors, experimental doses of human growth hormone. You can buy special prepackaged diets; memberships in Weight Watchers, Jenny Craig, and gyms. You can announce that you are "off carbs," without so much as raising an eyebrow. You can get liposuction; you can get lap band surgery or a gastric bypass. Since two out of three Americans are overweight, the subject is open game. When Oprah wheeled a wagon carrying sixty-seven pounds of fat onto her set in 1988, she launched a national conversation.

But rare is the woman who can openly declare that she's having trouble cutting back on booze. In this book, I distinguish between proven fact and conjecture, what is national habit, what is solid science, and what is rooted in our attitude toward alcohol. I also take a hard look at our country's traditional remedy for drinking problems, Alcoholics Anonymous, and how an increasing number of women are questioning its effectiveness and safety. Why are women drinking more than in previous eras, and what does it mean? Alcohol is a socially acceptable, legal way to muscle through the postfeminist, breadwinning, or stay-at-home life women lead. It's a drug women can respectably use in public and in private, even if it carries with it the risk of taking them under. It pops up in the headlines when a suburban mom kills seven others, including the kids she loves, but that's a gory headline. The real story is a silent, utterly bourgeois, and hiding-in-plain sight problem: How a lot of American women are hanging right over a cliff.

1 *Lush*

Solid statistics on women's drinking habits are hard to come by. In part, that's because all measures of potentially illicit behavior—sex, drugs, alcohol—are subject to the inherent inaccuracies of self-reporting. ("How many drinks a week?" "I don't know, Doc—maybe three or four.") There's also the historic indifference of the mostly male research community to focusing on gender differences in the science of disease. In recent years, however, a critical mass of credible studies have emerged that quantify the anecdotal evidence I had glimpsed in Portland and New York.

The findings are incontrovertible. By every quantitative measure, women are drinking more. They're being charged more often with drunk driving, they're more frequently measured with high concentrations of alcohol in their bloodstreams at the scene of car accidents, and they're more often treated in emergency rooms for being dangerously intoxicated. In the past decade, record numbers of women have sought treatment for alcohol abuse. And, in perhaps the most undeniable statistic of all, they are the consumers whose purchases are fueling steady growth in the sales of wine. Meanwhile, men's drinking, arrests for drunk driving, and alcohol purchases are flat, or even falling.

Contrary to the impression fostered by reality shows and *Gossip Girl,* young women alone are not responsible for these statistics. There are plenty of girls going wild on the nation's college campuses, but there is an even more striking trend of women in their thirties, forties, and fifties who are getting through their days of work, and nights with teething toddlers, trying teenagers, or sick parents, by hitting the bottle.

The risky habits of young women are well documented in articles, graphic memoirs, and cautionary TV specials. But their stories are more than just sad tales, or the school nurse's hyperbole: They are a serious public health concern. A national analysis of hospitalizations for alcohol overdose found that the rate of young females age eighteen to twenty-four jumped 50 percent between 1999 and 2008. In the same period, the rate for young men rose only 8 percent. The most alarming statistic was the sharp rise in the number of young women who turned up at hospitals having OD'd on both drugs and alcohol: That number more than doubled. Among young men, it stayed the same.

These data are part of a broader cultural shift in which drinking by women is seen as a proud rite of passage—or, at least, nothing to hide. I once shared a train ride with a loquacious college student who told me she was "practicing drinking" in advance of her planned spring break in Mexico. "It was my mom's idea, after I got sick over Christmas break from mixing rum with beer," she explained. "She doesn't want me making a fool of myself in Cabo, so we're working on getting my tolerance up."

Nothing like a little mother-daughter bonding—especially when gals with hollow legs get such respect. In 2011, students at Rutgers University chose *Jersey Shore*'s Snooki as a guest speaker on campus. The reality TV star—whose on-camera antics included blackout falls, an arrest for drunken and disorderly conduct, and the admission that she had often gotten so intoxicated she had woken up in garbage cans—was paid thirty-two thousand dollars for her talk. That was two thousand dollars more than writer Toni Morrison received for giving the school's commencement address six weeks later. Who needs guidance from a Nobel Prize winner when you can get advice like Snooki's? "Study hard," she told the crowd, "but party harder."

Middle-aged women aren't pounding shots or slurping tequila out of each other's belly buttons, but they, too, are drinking more than at any time in recent history. Their habits are different from those of their younger sisters. Their beverage of choice, after all, is wine, and their venue is less likely to be public.

In fact, the middle-class female predilection for wine seems like it's just a jolly hobby for time-stretched mothers. There are T-shirts with a spilled wineglass and the shorthand plea, "Not so loud, I had book club last night." Nearly 650,000 women follow "Moms Who Need Wine" on Facebook, and another 131,000 women are fans of the group called "OMG, I So Need a Glass of Wine or I'm Gonna Sell

My Kids." And the wine-swilling mom pops up as a cultural trope, from the highbrow to the mass market. In Jonathan Franzen's *Freedom*, Patty Berglund shuffles out for the morning papers every day with the "Chardonnay Splotch," the ruddy face of heavy drinkers. Nic, the driven doctor played by Annette Bening in *The Kids Are All Right*, downs her red wine a little too eagerly for her partner's taste. "You know what, Jules? I like my wine! Okay? So fucking sue me!" In the film *Smashed*, Kate, the fresh-faced first-grade teacher, wets her bed, throws up in front of her students, and drunkenly steals wine from a convenience store before she sobers up and leaves her drinking-buddy husband. Courteney Cox's *Cougar Town* character pours her daily red wine into giant vessels she calls Big Joe, Big Carl, and Big Lou. When Big Joe breaks, she holds a memorial service for its shards, tearfully recalling, "He was always there for me when I needed him." And drinking wine is so linked to the women of *Real Housewives* shows that three of the women it made famous—Bethenny Frankel, Ramona Singer, and Teresa Giudice—introduced their own brands.

In 2010, Gallup pollsters reported that nearly two-thirds of all American women drank regularly, a higher percentage than any other time in twenty-five years. Like many other studies around the world, Gallup found that drinking habits correlated directly with socioeconomic status. The more educated and well off a woman is, the more likely she is to imbibe. Catholics, atheists, agnostics, and those who identified themselves as non-Christians were also far more likely to drink than churchgoing Protestants.

White women are more likely to drink than women of other racial backgrounds, but that is changing, too. An analysis of the drinking habits of eighty-five thousand Americans between the early 1990s and the early 2000s found that the percentage of women who classified themselves as regular drinkers rose across the board. The number of white women drinkers increased 24 percent; Hispanics, 33 percent; and black women, 42 percent. (American Indian women were not included in this study. Because of the isolation of many Native American communities and the devastating role alcohol often plays in them, researchers typically study tribal alcohol use separately. Asian women were also not included; of all ethnic groups, they drink the least, perhaps because of a genetic intolerance that creates an uncomfortable flushing of the face and chest.)

Women are the wine industry's most enthusiastic customers. Despite the recession (or perhaps because of it), wine consumption in the U.S. continued to grow between the years 2009 and 2012, according to wine industry analysts.

Not all that wine is being decorously sipped. In 2012, the Centers for Disease Control and Prevention released a study that found 11 percent of American women binge drink regularly, about half the rate of men. Researchers define binge drinking as more than four drinks in two hours for women, and five drinks in two hours for men. While we are accustomed to the news of binge-drinking youths, the study revealed a surprising statistic: While more younger women binge drink, the highest frequency of binge drinking was among women ages sixty-five and older. On average, women over sixty-five overdid it six times every month, surpassing women in their twenties, who averaged four.

No surprise, then, that the number of women arrested for drunk driving rose nearly 30 percent in the nine years between

1998 and 2007. In California alone, between 1994 and 2009, that number doubled, going from 10.6 percent of all drivers to 21.2 percent. Women over forty had among the highest rates of arrest.

There is evidence that alcohol dependence among women is also rising precipitously. Two large national surveys of drinking habits, conducted in 1991 and 1992, and again in 2001 and 2002, found that women born between 1954 and 1963 had an 80 percent greater chance of developing dependence on alcohol than women who were born between 1944 and 1953. For men of those generations, the rate stayed flat.

The topic of women and alcohol is a relatively new one in academic research, with only a handful of experts around the country. Sharon Wilsnack, a distinguished professor of clinical neuroscience at the University of North Dakota School of Medicine and Health Sciences, became one of its pioneers as a graduate student at Harvard in the early 1970s. Though she has published hundreds of academic papers about women and alcohol, she is perhaps best known for the longitudinal studies of women's drinking she began conducting with her husband, sociologist Richard Wilsnack, in the early 1980s. Since then, the Wilsnacks have directed and analyzed in-depth, face-to-face interviews about drinking habits with more than eleven hundred women ages twenty-one to sixty-nine.

In the most recent evaluations of the study completed in 2002, Wilsnack noticed a startling shift: a substantial increase in the number and ways in which women reported intoxication. While the stigma of female drunkenness has faded since the first study in the early 1980s, Wilsnack is struck by the openness with which women today describe their drinking habits. She wasn't at all surprised by the frank talk of my train

partner, since she hears similar anecdotes at the lectures
gives on college campuses.

"There is a pattern of intentional drinking, with a w
plan behind it," she says. "Drinking on an empty stom
predrinking before going to a party or a bar; learning t
straight shots. They are very aware of their drinking, and
to manipulate it for maximum effect."

Wilsnack was struck by another new finding. In the e
1980s, one in ten women answered yes to the question: "
you concerned about your drinking?" In 2002, it was on
five.

That corresponds with what Rick Grucza, an epidem
ogist at Washington University in St. Louis, found in his
search on the generational shift of female alcohol depende
Because it's unlikely that anyone could accurately remem
how much they drank the previous decade, Grucza compa
how people in the same age groups responded to questi
about their consumption in two national surveys, the f
conducted in 1991–1992, and then ten years later. What
found among women was especially striking. When Gru
and his colleagues compared the two surveys, they saw a f
tening in consumption among younger and older men. T
opposite was true for women. "More women were drinki
and among those women, more women were becoming (
pendent," Grucza told me.

Grucza is a young guy, in his midforties, with a salt-ar
pepper goatee and a wry midwestern wit. He also partakes—
enjoy it," he told me—and steers clear of moralizing. He
careful not to place a value judgment on the behavioral n
rowing of the gender gap. For Grucza, the issue is how alcoh
disproportionately harms women.

Women of childbearing age are incessantly warned that alcohol poses a danger to the developing fetus, but nobody talks much about why women in general are more vulnerable to alcohol's toxic effects, too. They absorb more alcohol into their bloodstream than men because they have a higher percentage of body fat, and a lower percentage of water. Fat cells retain alcohol, but water dilutes it, so women drinking the same amount as men their size and weight become intoxicated more quickly than the men. Males also have more of the enzyme alcohol dehydrogenase that breaks down alcohol before it enters the bloodstream. This may be one reason alcohol-related liver and brain damage appears more quickly in heavy-drinking women than men. Alcohol-dependent women have death rates 50 to 100 percent higher than those of alcohol-dependent men, including those from suicide, liver cirrhosis, and alcohol-related accidents.

Increasingly, inebriated women get behind the wheel and careen into inanimate objects and other drivers. The tabloid photos of smashed starlets crashing their cars reflect a lot more than just celebrity culture: They're part of a gruesome wider trend. In California, the number of young women responsible for alcohol-related accidents jumped 116 percent between 1998 and 2007. It rose as well among young men, but only by 39 percent. While the number of U.S. drunk-driving deaths fell between 2001 and 2010, from 12,233 to 9,694, the number of female drivers responsible for them rose by 15 percent.

One way to measure the changes in women's drinking habits is in the frequency with which they seek help. Between 1992 and 2007, the number of middle-aged women who checked into rehab nearly tripled. That's especially telling: Disappearing for a month or more is difficult for any-

one, but it's especially tricky for women who have children
at home.

•   •   •

When it comes to alcohol treatment, there's growing evidence
that women are different as well. The antidote most commonly
recommended to problem drinkers in America—Alcoholics
Anonymous—is particularly ill-suited to women. A.A.'s
twelve-step approach instructs drinkers to surrender their
egos to a higher power, but it doesn't take a gender-studies
expert to know that women who drink too much aren't neces-
sarily suffering from an excess of hubris. The A.A. approach,
developed by men, for men, in the 1930s, is widely endorsed
by our medical and judicial systems and used by more than
90 percent of all treatment facilities in this country. No doubt
it has helped many people to a saner life. But an increasing
number of Americans, from addictions researchers to ex-A.A.
group leaders disturbed by some of the group's practices, are
challenging its toehold in U.S. society. They are frustrated
with the fact that many doctors, educators, and the general
public remain unaware of (or insist on ignoring) the numerous
scientific advances in the treatment of alcohol disorders.

Just as middle-aged women's drinking has been overlooked, so, too, has the success of recent evidence-based
treatments, methods whose efficacy has been determined by
rigorous scientific studies. A.A., a faith-based group whose
philandering, LSD-tripping cofounder, Bill Wilson, has
achieved the status of a demigod, remains embedded in public
minds as the best approach.

This tension over how to treat women who abuse alcohol is a new phenomenon, but the figure of boozy broads has deep roots in American history. In fact, the notion of the woman as the sober member of the household, the teetotaling mom, is relatively recent. Women who traveled from England on the *Mayflower* downed beer just like the male passengers, and women who trudged along on the Oregon Trail nipped from their whiskey jugs alongside the menfolk. How could they not? There was no safe drinking water, and when food supplies got low, alcohol had to fill in for calories' sake alone. Over time, however, women became leaders of the temperance movement, and by the early twentieth century, female imbibers fell into two categories. For one group of women, drinking was an act of rebellion, and a powerful declaration of modernity. For another, it was a shameful sin, a weakness to be hidden.

None of this thinking, now a century old but still deeply embedded in popular culture, takes into account what we now know about science, gender differences in the brain, and our peculiar history with alcohol itself. Nor does it presume to imagine the enormous ways in which our society has changed—particularly for women, who after all drink for reasons unimaginable to their colonial sisters.

2 We Are Women, Hear Us Pour

She was depressed. She was anxious. Because she was depressed and because she was anxious she drank too much. This was called medicating herself. Alcohol has its own well-known defects as a medication for depression but no one has ever suggested—ask any doctor—that it is not the most effective anti-anxiety agent yet known.

—Joan Didion, *Blue Nights*

The numbers seem clear enough. Women are drinking more. But data can only tell us so much. To understand *why* women are imbibing so frequently, we need to visit a place that is far less susceptible to quantitative assessment: the psyche of American women. Researchers believe that the predisposition toward alcohol abuse is a mix of factors, including learned behavior, genes, and psychology. My conversations around the country with women of varied ages, races, religions, and political outlooks returned again and again to a single theme. Drinking, they suggested, was a poorly chosen but understandable way to cope with the stresses of modern life.

Women are twice as likely to suffer from anxiety and depression as men, and they are more likely than men to treat their symptoms with alcohol, according to numerous studies. Other risk factors include a history of sexual abuse and bulimia, both of which also affect more women than men.

Alcohol ultimately depresses the working of the central nervous system, and heavy drinking compounds mood disorders, but initially, it delivers a quick cure for an ordinary day's blues. That's what makes it feel like an effective answer to life's rough patches, whether they're caused by financial worries, sleep problems during menopause, the illness of a parent, or sending the youngest kid off to college. It also helps stanch regretful ruminations. Many professional women I met had become mothers late in life and taken a hiatus from their careers, only to discover that motherhood wasn't quite as thrilling as they anticipated. They drank to cope with the boredom. The guilt. And above all, the jangling nerves.

Until recently, nobody even thought to look at how differently alcohol (and other mood-altering drugs) affected men's and women's brains. Some emerging neuroscience yields clues. In 2012, Yale researchers using advanced imaging equipment found that the areas of the brain associated with craving were activated by different cues in men and women. Stress was the predominant trigger in cocaine-dependent women, while visual cues, such as photos of the drug, stimulated cravings in the brains of cocaine-dependent men.

In a study she conducted as a graduate student at Harvard in the 1970s, Sharon Wilsnack discovered that alcohol generated different moods in men and women. Men reported feeling increasingly aggressive and powerful as they drank, while women said they felt calmer, less inhibited, and more easygoing.

These glimpses into alcohol's effects on women dovetail with much of my own reporting: I found women who functioned at a high level in high-pressure jobs, then came home and downed a bottle of wine while they made dinner. They'd hide the empty and open a second to share with their husbands, making it look as though they were just getting started. I met mothers who poured Baileys into their steel coffee cups as they drove their kids to elementary school, and more than a few who filled Poland Spring bottles with vodka and took them on their commutes.

If this sort of drinking sounds like a bourgeois problem, that's because largely it is. Alcohol problems aren't restricted to middle- and upper-middle-class women, but many of the enormous cultural shifts in our country have had an outsize impact on them.

The first change was an increased acceptance of female drinking: In the years after World War II, the growing American middle class turned cocktail hour into evening sacrament. In the proliferating suburbs, it was testament to civility. Men wanted to unwind after a hard day at the office and long commutes; women, too, craved some adult conversation after a long day of housework and childrearing. The kids trotted off to their rooms and the parents kicked back with martinis, manhattans, and mai tais. Like their bosses, career women often tippled themselves—and not just at the end of the day.

The late postwar era wasn't the first period in American history in which it was acceptable for women to imbibe (not by a long shot), but demure drinking had a powerful model at the highest level. Jacqueline Kennedy, an icon for modern new women, was educated, urbane, and sophisticated. Her style was a marked departure from the dour Bess Truman and the grandmotherly Mamie Eisenhower. She was a new American woman, inspiring tastes in fashion, art, food—and alcohol.

On Valentine's Day 1962, Jacqueline Kennedy guided television viewers through an hourlong tour of the White House, explaining architectural details and restored paintings. The tour was remarkable for a number of reasons, particularly because it was the first prime-time documentary directed specifically toward a female audience—many of whom were deeply anxious to get a glimpse into the life of this intriguing woman who, like them, was a young wife and mother.

When they saw the elegant place settings in the White House dining room, American women seized on a small piece of Kennedy glamour they could own for themselves. The camera panned across the gold-embossed official plates, and then lingered for a few seconds on the four adjacent crystal glasses. Mrs. Kennedy praised their graceful simplicity, mentioning offhandedly that they had come from a factory in West Virginia. This might seem like a minor detail, but fifty-six million Americans—three-quarters of all TV viewers—were watching. So much of the First Lady's life—her designer gowns, her summers on Cape Cod, her multilingual refinement—was out of reach. But anybody could buy her crystal, and the glass factory in Morgantown, West Virginia, struggled to keep up with the deluge of requests for its product. It would be years before they could fill all the orders.

The appetite for news of the Kennedys' style was insatiable. Even amid the anxiety of the Cold War and the Cuban missile crisis, the White House seemed determined to enjoy itself. When Letitia Baldrige, Mrs. Kennedy's social secretary, ordered the installation of a bar in the State Dining Room, early press reports were critical. But visitors soon adjusted to the elegance of the butlers who mixed drinks, circulated trays of champagne, and poured bourbon, scotch, and vodka. Under the Eisenhower administration, guests had to wait for an hour before dinner started with nothing stronger than fruit punch. By the time dinner rolled around, Baldrige later recalled, guests were in a lousy mood. The Kennedys' visitors strolled to the table in much higher spirits.

The glamorous first couple didn't invent cocktail parties, of course, but they were certainly part of the modern national Zeitgeist. Like all things in our free-market society, it was reinforced by innovative consumer goods, especially for women. Through the early 1960s, you couldn't open a magazine without seeing ads for cocktail dresses, cocktail aprons, cocktail rings.

But there were far more substantive changes afoot. Rick Grucza, the Washington University epidemiologist who has studied female drinking habits, correlates the rise in women's alcohol consumption to the increase in female college attendance. "Clearly there were many changes in the cultural environment for women born in the forties, fifties, and sixties compared to women born earlier," Grucza says. "They were freer to engage in a range of behaviors that were culturally or practically off-limits—and that includes excessive drinking."

Between 1940 and 1960, the number of women who had attended college, even for a year or two, rose sharply. Away from the watchful eyes of parents or spouses, women drank freely at mixers and fraternity parties, and continued the pattern as young wives. By 1963, Gallup pollsters found that 63 percent of all Americans were drinkers, a 15 percent increase from 1958. That survey doesn't show gender differences, but it's hard to imagine that the influx of college girls and Camelot didn't have something to do with the uptick.

By the mid-1970s, Gallup divided respondents by gender and age groups, and in 1977, the number of women who said they drank at least occasionally was up to 65 percent. The 1970s marked a high period for drinking in the United States after many states lowered their drinking age to eighteen. (Most had set the age at twenty-one after the repeal of Prohibition, but during the Vietnam War, many protesters argued about the absurdity of drafting eighteen-year-olds into army service when they couldn't yet buy beer. Highway fatalities skyrocketed, and by the early 1980s, the drinking age went back up to twenty-one.)

At the end of the 1970s, nearly half of all women were in the workforce, and the number of women graduating from college was nearing that of men. Many of these women began demanding a place in male-dominated careers like law, business, and journalism. They felt pressure to prove they were men's equals in the boardroom and at the bar. Grucza calls this voyage to a new world "immigrating."

These modern new women transformed American society in many ways. But modern American society would also transform them. Women's access to a wider world brought them greater achievements, greater equality, higher salaries, and more power. They also had a lot more of something once reserved mainly for men: stress. Luckily, there was a ladylike remedy for that modern affliction. Women didn't know it yet, but it would come in an ancient form: wine.

The migration of women into previously male bastions couldn't have arrived at a more opportune moment for the California wine industry.

In the decades after Prohibition's repeal, the state's wine producers had struggled to build a market for their product. Americans ate meat and potatoes, and like their Anglo-Saxon forebears, had a hankering for beer, or spirits that had been disguised with sweet mixers to mask the taste. They also consumed oceans of the sugary soda pop that had gained popularity during the country's dry spell: Coca-Cola, Dr Pepper, ginger ale, and 7Up, which had debuted originally as an antacid. Wine was the drink of the poor—for immigrants and skid-row drunks—or the well-traveled upper classes. For the rest of the country, exposure was limited to sips of the stuff during religious ceremonies: Catholics took syrupy wine at Communion, and Jews drank Manischewitz at the Sabbath table.

Not long after World War II, in a desperate attempt to introduce their product to Americans, vintners turned to Lucille Ball as a pitch woman. An ad in *Life* magazine shows Lucy with a frozen expression somewhere between a wince and a pained smile, clutching a highball full of California Burgundy over giant ice cubes. "Lucille Ball agrees!" Lucy helped move a lot of products, from cigarettes to face cream, but even she couldn't convince consumers to buy wine. The ad had a brief career.

Harvey Posert, one of the industry's first marketers, says Americans were deeply skeptical of wine as a routine refreshment. The Memphis-born, Yale-educated Posert came to San Francisco as vice president and western manager of the Edelman public relations agency after stints as a newspaperman and as a counterintelligence officer in the U.S. Army. When he was hired by the wine industry, he decided to conduct some research.

"Before we could get wine into people's houses, we had to get them to taste it," he says. "That wasn't so easy." In the mid-1960s, American moms were mixing up pitchers of Tang and Kool-Aid for their kids. Flavors of more adult refreshment weren't far off: This was the era of the Piña Colada, the White Russian, and the Pink Squirrel—Cool Whip cocktails! Posert hired ten representatives around the country to serve as informal wine ambassadors (my term, not his). He dispatched them to ski clubs, gourmet clubs, hiking clubs—anything that might reflect a desire for new experiences—and had his minions conduct wine tastings.

I met Posert a couple of times, and on this occasion we were in his airy, modern home in St. Helena, the epicenter of the California wine universe. Posert, now in his eighties, remains a Southern gentleman. He had poured me a flute of sparkling wine and a bourbon for himself—Posert discovered he is a "nontaster," unable to distinguish all but the bluntest of flavors—and we sat on the couch to chat before heading out for dinner.

The first several wine tastings, he recalled, were far from encouraging. Conveying the complexity of wine was going to take some work. The barriers seemed fundamental: Americans didn't like the taste. Red wine seemed "too strong." White wine seemed "sour." The hiking, cooking, and skiing tasters lacked even a language to describe what they disliked.

Still, the wine makers kept trying. "We used to joke that if we could just get a bottle of sherry into the kitchen, we'd be off," Posert says.

To the extent it was drunk at all, wine was a man's realm. Sommeliers were men, wine makers were men, wine merchants were men. In restaurants, wine lists (and the corks) were presented to men. Even ads were almost wholly masculine: Ludwig Stossel tottered around in lederhosen for Italian Swiss Colony wine, and Paul Masson promised not to serve wine before its time. Meanwhile, there was no guesswork to a gin and tonic.

Change arrived slowly, but got a boost from popular culture—especially from Julia Child's successful cooking show, *The French Chef*. As she lopped off fish heads and julienned carrots, she sipped wine liberally, and told Americans they could, too. Like wine growers, she, too, was from California, and she would become an important asset.

The Golden State itself embodied a new American style, the test kitchen for everything cool and interesting. Tourists flocked to the south to catch some of the Beach Boys' surfer vibe, and to visit Disneyland.

In the north, wine maker Robert Mondavi was creating a draw of his own with the 1966 opening of his majestic, Spanish-mission-style winery in Oakville. Designed by California architect Cliff May, the winery, bounded by the green Mayacama Mountains and shrouded with Pacific fog in the morning, was as distant from a modern amusement park as Europe itself. Mondavi envisioned a lifestyle—one he hoped Americans would adopt—based on the very old-world appreciation of wine, food, art, and music. He teamed with great chefs, including Child and Alice Waters, who had opened Chez Panisse in nearby Berkeley, and set upon producing wines he thought could compete with the great wines of Europe.

To make all this a commercial success, wine makers needed new customers, and they knew exactly who they were: American housewives. A pamphlet the wine industry circulated to grocers and liquor stores enlisted the merchants as allies in reaching her: "Wine is still new to Americans!" the undated copy reads. "*You* probably know at a glance what a wine bottle contains, but thousands of Americans might think it's syrup or salad oil. . . . That's why vendors need to 'Flag Customers Down' and explain why they want it."

Though three-quarters of wine buyers were male, the pamphlet said, the trend was changing. "Wine is used mostly in the home—on the dinner table and for entertaining. . . . The person who does the shopping for most of the home-used items is logically the one to do the wine buying. That person is the housewife."

It advised: "Before a housewife can be expected to buy a bottle of wine she must be given information concerning the use of that wine and a reason to use it. For example, 'Please your dinner guests—serve them this red table wine' tells her why she wants it."

In California, where laws allowed the sale of wine in supermarkets, Mondavi's marketing team hired housewives to stand at in-store tasting booths, offering other shoppers sips from bottles that would pair perfectly with what they planned to make for dinner. The saleswomen, often middle-aged, were friendly and reassuring. To young women especially, they helped make wine seem approachable.

Those young women would become an essential element in the astounding growth of wine sales. As the chief buyers of the growing middle class, with a new washing machine, dryer, and dishwasher, they had a lot of extra time on their hands—and a proliferating number of magazines to tell them how to fill it.

While Posert is a lively narrator, press clippings from those days give an even fuller picture of the campaign to get wine into America's kitchens. The University of California at Davis library has a vast collection of wine history, and its affable wine librarian, Axel Borg, directed me toward some remarkable evidence. In the early 1960s, food magazines carried a few timid mentions of serving wine to dinner guests, and there were odd suggestions here or there about the new craze in California: wine-tasting parties! Thumbing through a late-1960s *Ladies' Home Journal,* I saw an odd notation—a note about a "wine survey" the magazine had conducted in 1967. Borg dug up a reference, and a few weeks later, a copy arrived in the mail.

The report, called "Wine and Women: A Ladies' Home Journal Reader Reaction Bureau Report," looked about as official as something I might have typed in junior high, but the information it contained was an intriguing snapshot.

The magazine's interviewers had fanned out into ten cities, identifying a hundred women who said they drank wine at least once a month, and were confident enough around it to serve it to guests. The majority were in their thirties and forties, had graduated from or attended college, did not work outside the home, and had high-earning professional husbands. "The results of this study may be used to gain understanding of the attitudes behind the buying and serving of wines, with an eye to future sales," the report said.

The interviewers asked about the types of wine the women liked, what they believed about wine drinkers, and wine's importance. Overwhelmingly, the women found wine drinkers educated, cultured, successful people, and said they thought wine added "class." "It's nicer to serve than highballs," one woman wrote.

It's hard to say what the results of the report actually meant, and even Posert can't recall who might have commissioned it. But it was clear the industry was seeking early adopters, a term coined in 1962 that meant the initial customers of a company or product. These people, marketers believed, would go on to spread the word about a product as a trendsetter.

Many of the questions involved the women's willingness to attend, or throw, a wine-tasting party, and where they might get the training to do it.

It didn't take long for women to get comfortable. By the early 1970s, wine was ubiquitous. Magazines from *Vogue* to *Family Circle* covered the new fad, with tips on what to drink daily, and what to serve to your guests. Bridal magazines gave instructions on choosing the proper glasses for a registry, the right wines for the wedding reception, and which to have at home. For the uninitiated, there were directives: "Do You Know How to Order Wine in a Restaurant?" bellowed a headline in *Travel + Leisure*.

Wine was glamorous and hip, and it could also take the edge off. The Anti-Tension Diet in the February 1977 issue of *McCall's* gave wine a starring role. "Daily use of wine is recommended," it read. "A small amount of wine taken with meals is relaxing and promotes digestion, and table wines have another plus—since they're made from grapes, they're high in potassium."

In the 1970s, sixty-two million newspapers were sold in the United States every day, and publishers were expanding their feature sections in an attempt to reach a broader range of advertisers. Naturally, this included food and dining, a perfect outlet for the wine industry. It lavished its product on newspaper food writers, who were mostly women, when it hosted conferences on California cuisine. As food writers began to replace sloppy joe recipes with instructions for quiche and fondue, marketers believed they could help demystify wine, too. Advice from a trusted local voice felt like getting kitchen help from an aunt.

The marketing strategy soon branched beyond just housewives. Airlines offered California wines on flights to San Francisco and Los Angeles, exposing neophytes to their first sips of Golden State glamour. In buttoned-down Washington, D.C., California senators and congressmen held evening wine-tasting parties that drew hundreds of thirsty interns, who in turn began buying wine themselves. More than two hundred colleges staged tastings, and industry representatives introduced wine at more than forty-five hundred women's groups, from grandmotherly garden societies to political clubs.

"Anything to get people to taste it, to familiarize themselves," Posert says. "We thought of as many ways as we could."

For Margrit Biever, who would become Mondavi's second wife, selling wine seemed like second nature. The Swiss-born Biever had arrived in Napa as a young army wife with three children. Bored at home once her children were in school, she took a job at the winery in 1967, leading crowds through tasting rooms with her considerable charm. A student of art, a lover of music, an accomplished, effortless chef and gardener, fluent in seven languages, Biever embodied the lifestyle Mondavi had both envisioned and hoped to project with his product. The two fell in love, marrying in 1980.

At lunch recently in St. Helena, Biever Mondavi entered the restaurant in a pink sweater and red patent leather peep toes. She sat back in a booth across from me, addressing one acquaintance in Spanish, another in Japanese, and brushed her chic blond bob back from her face as she daintily dipped her sushi into soy sauce. As a child, she says, she attended La Scala twice a year, and learned to enjoy wine from her father's cherished wine cellar. "My father gave my brother, sister, and me an appreciation of which Beaujolais or Fendant paired well with what," she recalls. "He told us great stories about the wines, the regions they came from, even the vintages. Wine was something special, and I knew it could be in America, too."

Her arrival at Mondavi would help cement the transformation. "What a wonderful time those days were!" she says. "It was so exciting, helping explain the wine, the tastes, how to pair it. It was helping open another world, and it was wonderful!" Once, as the winery neared closing time, a group of hippies arrived in a beat-up van. "Everyone was a little leery of them—you know, their beards, their long hair," she says. "Napa Valley in the early 1970s was still a very traditional place." Biever led the group through the tasting rooms, offering sips from reserve bottles as her colleagues grumbled. An hour later, her group bought eight hundred dollars' worth of wine—the equivalent of forty-two hundred dollars today. "Wine is life," she says. "Passion! Beauty! Joy! Fun!"

By the late 1970s, California wines were earning respect outside the U.S., even winning two blind taste tests at a Paris competition. They helped put traditional little Napa on the map for good: In just one decade, Americans had doubled their wine consumption, from 267 million gallons in 1970 to 480 million in 1980.

Behind the scenes, California's wine makers were unintentionally tweaking their product in ways that made it even more appealing to women. European wine making was ruled by a strict code of tradition and *terroir*, the French term for the special characteristics that the geography, geology, and climate of a certain place bestow upon certain crops. Americans, starting almost from scratch after Prohibition, felt free to experiment with how best to turn their grapes into a likable product. At the University of California at Davis, wine makers tried a variety of techniques, using different oak barrels and fermentation processes that could influence flavor. Though wine making was predominantly male, in the changing social climate of California, it had attracted bright young women.

One was a young scientist named Zelma Long, the second woman to be awarded a master's in enology and viticulture from Davis. In 1970, she landed a job as one of the country's first female wine makers at Mondavi's winery. Long, who was reared in the small town of The Dalles, Oregon, had started her career as a dietitian, but quickly grew bored with the restrictive regimens she felt she had to recommend for her diabetic and hypertensive patients. Long had grown up in a Swedish American household on simple, hearty food she recalls as subtly delicious. She was drawn to Davis, an innovator in the evolving field of sensory science—how humans responded to the appearance, flavors, and aromas of food, drink, and other substances, including tobacco. (As Americans consumed more packaged and canned foods, by then easily transportable on the expanding interstate highway system, manufacturers needed researchers to investigate the best ways to preserve flavor and consistency.)

When Long arrived at Mondavi, she almost couldn't believe her luck. She was immersed in—indeed, part of—the transformation of the American table even as it was occurring. One of the wines Long began to experiment with was chardonnay, which had gone from virtually no plantings of the grape in the mid-1960s to overnight popularity.

Taste tests from the early California whites were universally negative—they were too dry and thin for American taste buds, accustomed, as they were, to sugary drinks. Chardonnay, a thick-skinned grape originating in eastern France, had shown promise as one that adapted easily to many climates, and it thrived in Napa. By using a process called malolactic fermentation, wine makers can reduce tartness and turn the natural green fruit into soft, buttery flavors.

Long was among a handful of vintners who helped perfect a golden, velvety chardonnay that American women liked immediately. "For people who were new to wine, it had a rich, satiny, smooth texture. On top of that, it had these vanilla, apple, spicy scents that were already familiar, like apple pie," says Long, who has become an admired wine maker and business owner. She now works as a consultant with wineries around the globe. "It was just an easy wine, and people liked it." It also sounded fancy, even feminine. It was easy to say, easy to drink, and had fewer astringent tannins than, say, the cabernet sauvignons the region was also developing.

Sales of chardonnay skyrocketed, and women emerged as its top consumers. In the 1980s, it became the thinking woman's drink, especially for those who were born in the early part of the baby boom. As that group of women matured, they drove consumer markets with their tastes. They wore shoulder pads and business suits, and they drank chardonnay. It seemed thoughtful, intelligent, serious, and markedly different from the heavy cocktails of their parents' generation. Press reports began to emphasize how healthy wine's effects were (and in moderation, they can be). For a brief period, until advertising rules restricted the use of the vague word "light" in promoting lower-calorie foods, white wine was also touted as an alcoholic diet drink, especially if you mixed it with ice and seltzer. That claim proved difficult to substantiate: absent dilution, and depending on its alcohol content, white wine has about five fewer calories per ounce than red. That would give a small glass of white wine about 100 calories; a small glass of red, 120. But for many years, women associated white wine with dietary restraint.

It is impossible to gauge precisely how much women buyers helped boost the early sales. The wine industry only began analyzing the gender of its consumers in the mid-1990s, and by then, women made up the majority of its buyers.

It is certainly in their kitchens. Today, women buy nearly two-thirds of the 784 million gallons of the wine sold in this country, and they drink 70 percent of what they buy.

•　　•　　•

The wine industry's efforts to market its product to women came at a pivotal moment in America's ever-changing gender roles. By the 1980s, the struggle for women's rights had brought some remarkable strides. An Arizona rancher took her place beside eight elderly men on the nation's Supreme Court. One of the nation's political parties chose a woman as its vice presidential candidate. Sally Ride circled the earth. Women were graduating from college with degrees in math, science, and engineering in unprecedented numbers.

They didn't need to go to frat parties to drink, since they lived alongside boys in college dorms across the country. The beer bongs were always within reach, along with treacly Tia

Maria and wine coolers. That kind of drinking was just kid stuff: nothing serious. It continued on through first jobs, when the women would cluster with colleagues at happy hour for free food and cheap drinks. Even if the women woke up most mornings in a fitful self-loathing start, there were *possibilities*. As the president of my university told young women when Ride was launched into space, orbit was our destiny!

For a decade or more, their lives were on track: a solid career, a steady marriage, children. They could do it all—manage their jobs *and* immerse themselves in their children. They would bake birthday cakes from scratch; they would go to every swim meet. They would be there, period. No Carnation Instant Breakfast mothering for them.

But somehow, something changed. Those same young women, so full of determination, found themselves scaling back their dreams: for running the English Department, for winning a Pulitzer, for becoming CEO. Aspirations somehow dropped to the bottom of the grocery bags that used to be plastic bottles. The women haven't even made good on their intention to compost.

When they are honest about it—and it is hard to be, because sometimes it's too painful to look—the women realize they are doing the same chores as their mothers. They scale back at work, or maybe even take off a few years, and before long, the women find themselves isolated, responsible not only for care of the children but for most details of their lives: trips to the doctor when the baby has croup; combing through tangled braids on the lookout for lice; making appointments with the orthodontist. They didn't plan it that way, but that's how it happened. Resentment creeps up, imperceptibly, not the least of which stems from the fact that the closet full of size-six clothes don't fit a size-eight body. They haven't had more than social drinks in years—all that time pregnant or nursing, no way. But then they remember how it made them feel. The fun of it. What would be wrong with a little wine now and then?

And so the drink becomes the release valve, for so many things. For Memorial Day. For the Fourth of July. For Halloween—especially Halloween, when women gather with other moms for "trick-or-drinking." And summer, when they are all at the beach, and the beers come out at noon. Giggle, giggle. Mommy's right here!

The drinks kept coming, especially when parents got sick, when teenagers got testy, when promotions were handed to younger, prettier women who tweet. If the women had had hold of the torch, they might be ready to pass it. But expectations exceeded reality, and they never held on to it.

Psychologist Bruce Alexander, a Canadian addiction expert, believes the unrelenting pressures of our modern capitalist society have created the emotional, psychological, and spiritual dislocation that triggers alcohol abuse. Modern society distances people from their extended families and propels a desire for an increasing number of goods—particularly technological ones—that in the end isolate them even more. Lacking the intimate ties necessary for humans to live happily, a growing number of people around the world turn to chemical crutches. Alexander is also a student of history, which he used to link to his work as an addiction psychologist. The more he examined history, the more Alexander became convinced that the breathtaking pace of modern economic and social change has left an emotional, physical, and spiritual void so profound that it triggers excess drinking.

The richer societies get, Alexander argues, the more their addiction problems multiply—and so far, our responses to treating them have been only nominally successful. A century ago, society blamed addiction on a person's weak moral character. In the 1940s and '50s, this belief was replaced by the idea that addiction was "brain disease," and it was one that seeped into the public consciousness. Alexander doesn't reject the idea that some people may have biological and psychological vulnerabilities that predispose them toward chemical dependence. But, he argues, addiction is also an adaptation to the pressures and fragmentation of modern life—and above all, a social problem, not an individual one.

Alexander's views are a compelling explanation of why twenty-first-century women have emerged as such heavy drinkers. Our fractured modern society subjects everyone to immense pressures, but it spawns competition that is particularly grueling near the top of social hierarchies—especially those in affluent communities. Absent the support of an extended family and a long-standing community, these deracinated American women—Grucza's immigrants to male culture—suffer without a spiritual safety net. Regardless of their professional achievements, they still do the lion's share of domestic chores in the United States. A quick fix for the frustration that this can engender is just a bottle away.

Consider the time, long ago, before mothers were assigned snacks for children famished by forty-minute soccer games. Saturdays weren't vaporized by long-distance drives to "travel" soccer (or lacrosse, or hockey), since sports were school functions and practice was after school. Perhaps more important, women lived near their own parents, sisters, brothers, in-laws, or cousins, whom the school secretary recognized as next of kin. There was no need to fill out multipage forms detailing one's relationship to emergency contacts, with slots for their cell, work, and home phone numbers. Everyone knew everyone, and if children were sick, someone could come pick them up. A few generations ago, homework assignments rarely required (or would have prompted) parental help, with rushed trips to Staples for foam boards.

While women surely have fretted forever about aging, they were resigned to the inevitable wrinkles in the end. Today, aging can feel a lot like a decision. Forget Botox: Magazine ads make us wonder about Radiesse, Juvederm, the length of our eyelashes. Middle-aged starlets tweet photos of themselves in bikinis; blond sixty-something celebrities boast of their renewed libido, thanks to HGH, the human growth hormone. This is all just background chatter in the bête noire of middle- and upper-middle-class anxiety: college applications. What if a son doesn't bring up his critical reading score in the SAT? What if a daughter only gets into her "safety" school? What if the hired school getter-inner is steering you all wrong? Did you read this blog? Did you read that book? Does your kid have enough work experience? Any work experience? There is nothing wrong with state schools.

Is there?

●　　●　　●

It is easy to see these luxury anxieties as unseemly complaints by people who enjoy substantial benefits from our consumer society. But my experiences—and reporting—show there is a profound disquiet playing out in the work and home lives of these women, in the vise between their families and their hopes. For the six years we lived in Portland, Oregon, my kids played with neighborhood kids, climbing trees and riding their bikes to the corner store for Popsicles. Across the country, in the New Jersey suburb where I live now, freedom is much more limited. In the densely populated East, competition for the brass ring of college is greater. And time—free time—is the first casualty. Sociologist Annette Lareau describes this phenomenon as "concerted cultivation" by upper-middle-class parents. The effects on kids are documented in the poignant film *Race to Nowhere,* which features the parents of a thirteen-year-old girl who killed herself after she got a bad math grade. We see it in Richard Louv's powerful book lamenting housebound children, *Last Child in the Woods.*

The impact of this self-induced stress on mothers is palpable. A few years ago, Valerie Ramey, an economics professor at the University of California's San Diego campus, found herself spending an increasing amount of her nonworking, alleged free time engaged in child-related activities. Being a quantitative sort, she immediately wondered: How common is this?

It was a natural question for Ramey, an economist whose specialty, among other topics, is how Americans use their time. I met her on a drizzly fall day, rare in San Diego, for a long afternoon. She is small and athletic, with a trim build, long, thick blond hair she inherited from her Swedish ancestors, and a gentle, youthful face. Ramey, now in her early fifties, grew up in the Panama Canal Zone, where her father worked as an electrician. She graduated summa cum laude with a double major from the University of Arizona, and got her Ph.D.

at Stanford University. Her midwestern parents instilled in Ramey a love of books, adventure, and the abiding sense that American society was a meritocracy in which hard work was rewarded.

And so Ramey worked hard. She married a fellow economist, Garey Ramey, in her midtwenties, and had her first child, Sean, a few years later. The couple bought their first house, in a working-class San Diego neighborhood, where most of their neighbors were immigrant families.

When Sean approached middle school, the family moved to a more affluent neighborhood near campus, where schools offered more opportunities. But perhaps the biggest difference in their new location was the daytime milieu: Most of the mothers were home during the day. As the Rameys' two children made friends, she met their mothers. The new neighbors fretted openly about how good grades were no longer sufficient in securing a bright future. It was essential, the women told Ramey, that kids be involved in a range of activities in order to earn a spot at the country's top schools.

As an academic, Ramey was well aware of the increasing selectivity of American universities, but the anxious talk made her snap into action. She enrolled her daughter in Brownies and softball. She baked cookies, gave rides, arranged rides. She insisted that her extroverted, mechanically minded son join the water polo team, even though he had despised the other sports she had suggested he try—Pop Warner football, baseball, soccer. After school, father and son drove to and from practice, while Ramey and her daughter would race to softball and Brownies. Garey and Sean would have much preferred to spend more time at their favorite activities together—making airplane and ship models, or playing strategic board games—

but Ramey kept urging her son to keep up with sports. Sports, sports, sports.

Meanwhile, Ramey's daughter developed a passion for horseback riding. The stables were far, and the riding commitment was a minimum of six hours a week. After all her talk about the importance of being well rounded, Ramey didn't feel like she was in a position to discourage this new athletic interest.

But one day, after a particularly hectic workweek, Ramey found herself in a stall next to her daughter. Her back ached from hauling the heavy saddle out of the trunk, and as she bent to pitch hay and manure she found herself flat-out furious. What the hell was she doing heaving horse manure when she could be home poring over cookbooks—*her* passion? Reading a novel? Dancing? "My husband had asked me, 'Why are you doing all this stuff?' I said, 'Because you have to!' His response was, 'Says who?'"

The baking and the driving, though, were precisely what many of her new neighbors were doing. Many had graduate degrees and had reached enviable status in their fields, particularly law and business. Unlike Ramey, though, many had left their jobs, their tailored clothing, and their access to high-speed copiers because they needed more time to drive their kids to art class and swim meets. "I couldn't understand why anyone would make such a decision," she said. At first, she assumed the answer was simple economics: that the male overwhelmingly outearned the woman, or had huge demands on his schedule.

The Rameys were not in that position. While comfortable, their lifestyle was far from lavish. And the family often bickered—over who did what, whose turn it was do the dishes or clean the pool—a direct result of the lack of time. Her son, especially, complained about his grueling water polo schedule. Her daughter asked if she could stop playing softball. Ramey did not back down. Kids had to play sports! Everyone said it! "What is happening?" she asked out loud one evening as she poured herself a second glass of zinfandel. "What am I doing?"

"I'll tell you what you're doing," her husband said gently. "I know you're competitive, but these other mothers are competing to see who is spoiling their children the most. You're always saying that you don't want spoiled, entitled kids." He took a deep breath. "Is this one you really want to win?"

She came, she says, to her senses—and pulled back. "Make your own choices," she told her kids.

Ramey saw changes in her family immediately. Her son became involved in their neighborhood Catholic church (which was only a block from home and required no driving), where he led a youth group and became involved with literacy programs for immigrant families. "He was relieved to do what he wanted, not what I thought was a good idea for his college application," Ramey says. (He is now a graduate student at Stanford.) Her daughter, an animal lover, transferred her passion for horses to the local shelter, and used her skills as a photographer to help shoot pictures of creatures that needed homes. Rather than squander hours on the freeway, she spent time developing her own photographs in a makeshift studio she made with her dad. (She is now a student at the University of California at Berkeley.)

Valerie, too, was relieved, turning more to the activities that she found relaxing: cooking, dancing, reading. (She enjoys wine, but never steps beyond what she calls the "law of diminishing returns"—where pleasure is replaced by a hangover, or the inability to grade papers at night.) As her son moved through his high school years, students around him kept an exhausting pace. Was this nonstop enrichment, abetted by mothers who had quit their jobs or cut back their work hours, a fad that affected only their San Diego zip code? Together, Valerie and Garey, an economic theorist at UCSD, decided to investigate.

By studying Bureau of Labor Statistics data from 1965 to 2007, the Rameys discovered a national trend: For all the upper-middle-class frenzy about the never-ending workday, the researchers found that the amount of time dedicated to child care increased dramatically in the past fifteen years, even as the number of children in households dropped. The Rameys' analysis revealed another detail: Parents reported that their child-care demands increased as their kids grew older.

On average, college-educated women in 2007 spent twenty-two hours per week on child care, an increase of nine hours more than women in the mid-1990s; women without college educations had an increase of five hours, from eleven to sixteen. Meanwhile, college-educated fathers increased the time they spent with their kids to ten hours from four, while fathers without a college degree logged a four-hour increase, up to eight from four hours in the 1990s. Overwhelmingly, the time-use category with the biggest upswing was "chauffeuring."

What could account for this huge shift? The government sample hadn't changed over the years, and the time jump wasn't attributable to a rise in income. Crime, which prompts parents to keep closer tabs on their kids, had dropped from its all-time high in the early 1990s. Workplace flexibility hadn't increased. Nor had the mothers suddenly developed an overwhelming desire for late-afternoon driving. In fact, on the enjoyment scale, women ranked this kind of "child care" below cooking, cleaning, and folding laundry. The hours have more than a social and emotional impact: They come at an economic cost, too. The Rameys calculated that they account for more than $300 billion of forgone wages a year.

"We were so puzzled," Ramey says. "Why were women with master's degrees quitting their jobs to drive their kids around? Why would they have made that decision?" The Rameys concluded that the women in their neighborhood were part of a national trend, and that the increased scarcity of college slots has heightened rivalry among parents, taking the form of more hours spent on college preparatory activities. "In other words, the rise in child-care time resulted from a 'rug rat race' for admission to good colleges," they wrote.

To test their hypothesis, the Rameys compared child-care data in the United States and Canada, since the countries share many social trends. In Canada, however, college admissions are less competitive. In addition, most cities and towns have free community centers where kids play hockey and basketball or swim; buses, not parents, transport children there from school. The Rameys found that the amount of time parents spent on child care in Canada remained the same during the past two decades.

Ramey does not see the American trend reversing itself anytime soon. "I think a lot of women feel they are really making the best decision for their children," she says.

But what about their own lives? Do these mothers feel fulfilled by the successes of their children—or resentful of their own sacrifices? Evidence suggests that the pattern is helping to produce a generation of very unhappy women. According to a 2009 study released by two Wharton School economists, data from the government's General Social Survey revealed that women rated their own happiness at the lowest level in thirty-five years. Each year, the survey includes a representative sample of fifteen hundred men and women of all ages, races, marital status, and educational and income levels, for a total of fifty thousand people so far.

Regardless of whether they work or stay home, are single or married, have graduate degrees or high-school diplomas, women rated feeling bleak about the state of their lives. And overall, mothers had the gloomiest outlooks of anybody.

By comparison, men responded to the same survey with downright giddiness compared to women.

The study's authors, economists Betsey Stevenson and Justin Wolfers, suggested that men might feel less of a burden because they no longer carry the sole financial responsibility for the household. They now work less and relax more. With divorce now commonplace, men are free to leave unhappy marriages. (So are women, but more than two-thirds of mothers are awarded sole or primary custody after a divorce.)

Women, on the other hand, feel the loss of social and family cohesion their mothers enjoyed more acutely. They also report more anxiety than previous generations: In the 1970s, women were at once more optimistic about the future and had lower expectations for what they might achieve. Today, they rate a low level of perceived success both as mothers and as professionals. And, as the Rameys demonstrated, women dislike how they spend their leisure time.

There are a number of theories for why women report such unhappiness. Perhaps earning a higher income has led to greater financial pressures—a bigger mortgage, or unaffordable private school tuitions. Or maybe women are judging their lives against a new frame of reference. Today, a woman who is dismayed at being passed over for company vice president might report more dissatisfaction than her predecessors, who compared themselves to fellow homemakers. Despite their increased opportunities, many women feel they still haven't measured up. "Or," Stevenson and Wolfers conclude, "women may simply find the complexity and increased pressure in their modern lives to have come at the cost of happiness."

For many women, the unfulfilling, stressful tasks of running a household, mixed with the regret of lost opportunities and the loneliness of social isolation, add up to a 750-milliliter reason to drink. Of course, women don't just turn to wine, or even just alcohol. The leading character on the Showtime drama *Nurse Jackie* hoards, pops, and snorts pain pills. They don't smell, and they're easy to hide. Unlike alcohol, though, they are hard to get: They require prescriptions, pharmacies, and the complicated underworld of shady pain-management doctors who don't ask questions.

Wine is far easier. It's civilizing. It's *good* for us. We're supposed to drink it, right? What's wrong with a group of gals enjoying their chardonnay? The problem, of course, arises when the drinking becomes something more than a festive night out, when women begin downing their wine urgently, on empty stomachs. These women are not sipping a glass or two with dinner to relax. They are building their days around drinking time. Which for some begins as soon as the youngest child gets on the bus.

3 *I Have to See a Man about a Dog*

In the ebb—but mostly flow—of booze in America, liberal drinking among women is nothing new. The Pilgrims packed more beer than water on the *Mayflower,* landing in Plymouth when supplies got low. Alcohol was essential for hydration, and during lean times, calories. It disinfected wounds and eased pains from childbirth to abscessed teeth. No one ate mashed potatoes at the first Thanksgiving, but there were seconds and thirds of beer, brandy, rum, and gin.

In colonial America, booze making was women's work. In addition to the usual domestic chores of cleaning, sewing, and cooking, colonial women prepared the alcoholic drinks their families drank at breakfast, lunch, and dinner. They used fermented apples to make cider, rotting peaches to make brandy, and a drink called "perry" from pears. They made wine out of celery and onions and brewed beer out of pumpkin and spruce. They made wassail. They concocted a drink called "flip": a pint of beer mixed with sugar and molasses, topped off with a shot of rum and heated with a red-hot poker. Even babies drank home brew in tin or pewter "nursers," bottle-shaped vessels with crude spouts.

By the early 1700s, northern colonies were distilling their own rum with sugar from the Caribbean, and it became the most popular beverage in the taverns central to colonial life. Taverns welcomed both men and women, and were orderly meeting places to discuss politics and conduct business, read the newspaper, and exchange local gossip. But the main draw was drink, especially rum. Everybody partook—even the Puritans. We often dismiss negative attitudes toward alcohol as "puritanical," but in fact it was drunkenness, not drinking, the Puritan preachers condemned. On frigid Sunday mornings, Puritan worshipers filed into the pubs built adjacent to their churches so they could warm their hands by the tavern's fire— and their bellies with rum—before services.

By the mid-1700s, rum consumption was beginning to present some social problems. The settlers were accustomed to downing big mugs of low-alcohol cider and beer, and treated rum as if it were just the same. But it had five times the alcohol content, and drunkenness grew to be so common that the colonists developed more than two hundred expressions to describe various states of inebriation. Ben Franklin published a list of them in an article called "The Drinker's Dictionary."

To be sure, there weren't a lot of nonalcoholic choices. Milk was available only during calving season, and required proximity to farms. Water lacked flavor, especially to taste buds accustomed to more exciting refreshment. It was also dangerous. Wells were easily contaminated by human or animal waste, and settlers living near the seashore, as most did, had to cope with brackish water that flowed into their streams during storms. Tea and coffee were luxuries for the wealthy alone.

It's fair to say that booze played a part in fueling the American Revolution. Paul Revere nipped rum during his midnight ride. Jefferson drank three or four glasses of wine a night. John Adams started every morning with a tankard of hard cider, and George Washington set up a Mount Vernon whiskey distillery in the waning days of his presidency.

Like everybody else, women drank plenty, too.

As it turns out, Martha Washington was more than just the first First Lady: She was also a Founding Mixologist. In a collection of recipes she gave to her granddaughter as a wedding gift, she lists instructions for sausage, stews, and puddings. But she really gets serious with her recommendations for boozy drinks. Rum punches, berry wines, meads, and liqueurs were crucial for any great party, Martha wrote. She also issued some practical advice: Birch wine could prevent kidney stones, poppy seeds soaked in spirits could relieve a hangover, and regular doses of an herbal cordial called aqua mirabilis was good for fighting the blues: "It disperseth melancholly & causeth cheerfulness."

But this one makes me laugh out loud every time I read it:

Capon Ale

Take an old capon with yellow leggs. Pu(ll) him and crush ye bones but keep ye scin whol(e) & then take an ounce of

*carraway seeds and an ounce of anny seeds and two ounces
of har(ts) horne and one handful of rosemary tops, a piece or
two of mace and a leamon pill. sow all these into ye bellie of
your capon and chop him into a hot mash, or hot water, and
put him into two gallons of strong ale when it is working. . . .
This ale is good for any who are in a consumption & it is
restorative for any other weakness.*

Nobody took much note of women's drinking in the eighteenth century, unless they really overdid it. Betsy Ross's sister was expelled from her Friends meetinghouse for "excessive use of strong drink." During the Revolutionary War, General Henry Knox got regular updates from the Connecticut landlord who was renting his home to Knox's young wife, Lucy. She and her army-wife roommate treated the place like it was a frat house. The landlord complained that the women had smashed his crockery, and emptied his cellar of twenty-five gallons of rum.

Liquor did have its critics, and one of the most outspoken was Benjamin Rush, a doctor who signed the Declaration of Independence. Rush wrote a pamphlet about the effects of alcohol in which he suggested that wine and beer could be beneficial in moderation, but that distilled spirits resulted only in poor mental and physical consequences.

From a public health standpoint, Rush was a pioneer in understanding, and communicating, the impact of prolonged excess. Tucked into his treatise was an argument that abstinence was the only cure for compulsive drinking. Educators and clergy embraced his message, but Americans didn't. The four decades after the Revolutionary War were tumultuous years of high national debt, inflation, unemployment, expansion, and immigration—and the country relied on copious amounts of booze to get through it.

In his investigation of early American drinking, historian W. J. Rorabaugh estimated that between the 1790s and the 1830s, every man, woman, and child over the age of fifteen consumed about six and a half gallons of pure alcohol a year, a level not reached before or since. Drinking crossed gender, class, and racial boundaries. Whites introduced American Indians to alcohol, to devastating effect. And though booze was largely off-limits to enslaved Africans, plantation owners shared their supplies on holidays.

In the early years of the republic, the burgeoning East was blotto: Buffalo, transformed by the completion of the Erie Canal in 1825, had a saloon for every eighty-four men, women, and children. New York State had a distillery for every fourteen hundred residents.

On the vast and expanding frontier, stills for barley, corn, and rye marked every property. Western farm, lumber, and mining towns were packed with saloons, which had become central to the lonely and uncertain life of the migrants who ventured there. "Bread is considered the staff of life," wrote a thirteen-year-old Missouri girl who arrived in a Colorado mining town in the 1860s. "Whisky the life itself."

I thought about one of my own great-great-grandmothers, whose name I could not have invented even for purposes of this book. Martha Ann Drinkard traveled from Missouri to Oregon in 1865, walking—while pregnant—from a hardscrabble present into a frighteningly uncertain future with four children in tow. Pioneers on the Oregon Trail packed between five and ten gallons of whiskey onto their wagons for medicinal use (and calories). Martha's prairie schooner is the centerpiece of a small pioneer museum in Brownsville, Oregon, that outlived any journal in which she may have recorded her thoughts.

But many women on the trail wrote of hitting the bottle from time to time. What else could quell the rootless uncertainty, the longing of homesickness? How else to cope with the grief of burying children or spouses who dropped dead of cholera the same day they got sick? Drink was adaptation, and it is as clear as the names of landmarks where I grew up: Whiskey Creek, Whiskey Lake, Whiskey Butte. Those are just some gulches, rivers, and runs named after the liquor in my home state. From Tennessee to Alaska, there are nearly five hundred more.

•   •   •

In the early years of the country, men outnumbered women by a significant margin. While women were considered the "weaker sex," their skills as midwives and seamstresses were essential, and therefore valued, in the new society. They lacked economic, political, and legal rights, but in the colonial era women were nevertheless important figures in the chief unit of the colonial economy: the family. The work required to sustain it demanded that all members step in wherever they were needed, whether it was driving a plow horse or delivering livestock. Though it didn't exclude love, colonial marriage was a business partnership first.

As the economy of the East and Midwest shifted from agriculture to manufacturing in the first part of the nineteenth century, the white, nonimmigrant women who lived there found themselves with a dwindling realm of influence. Males, as wage earners or business owners, became families' sole breadwinners. New social values restricted women to house-keeping, childrearing, and religious education, with no role in their financial futures. A new generation of women were now isolated in their homes.

The economic shift was accompanied by a religious revival called the Second Great Awakening. Starting in the 1820s, Protestant preachers fanned throughout the growing frontier seeking converts. They emphasized personal salvation and the pressing need to clean up the country's social ills in preparation for the return of Christ. Nearly all of the denominations denounced slavery, prostitution, and gambling. But most saved their most powerful vitriol for the evils of alcohol. The rapidly growing Methodist, Baptist, and Congregationalist churches demanded congregants give up alcohol before they could join. (This was made possible by the expansion of public filtering systems, which had eased the replacement of booze with clean drinking water.)

The stark message of the religious revival—hell's fires for the wicked, the promise of heaven for the virtuous—struck an especially sharp chord with middle-class women, who were struggling to articulate their roles in the new social order. Technological advances were building a new country, but the prevailing ideology made clear that it would fall to women to civilize it.

Mass communications helped show them how. Unlike the friendly wine-drinking tips in 1970s publications, nineteenth-century women's magazines were loaded with morality lessons. They stressed the dangerous nature of the competitive industrial world, and instructed readers to create an ethical haven at home. Architects of these new "separate spheres" argued that women could demonstrate their virtuousness by accepting these strict divisions of labor.

The most popular guidance came in a magazine called *Godey's Lady's Book,* which ran a mix of poems, articles, editorials, and serialized novels, often written by women. It had a circulation of 150,000 in the 1840s, but its readership was far higher than that. Women who couldn't afford the cost of a subscription joined clubs in order to share the magazine and discuss its contents. Its editor, Sarah Hale, an antislavery novelist, poet, and author of the nursery rhyme "Mary Had a Little Lamb," had an Oprah-like influence on her middle-class readers in matters of taste, etiquette, and opinion.

Hale used her forty-year reign at *Godey's* to rally support for her favorite causes, and her efforts were remarkably fruitful. The publication of a treatise on women's education generated the founding of a dozen girls' schools and colleges. She campaigned five presidents for the proclamation of Thanksgiving as a national holiday, finally succeeding with Lincoln. When she serialized T. S. Arthur's antialcohol novel, *Ten Nights in a Bar-Room and What I Saw There,* she effectively ensured that the topic would, in today's terms, go viral.

The book describes the downfall of a small town after the opening of its first tavern. None of its characters is immune from alcohol's destruction, regardless of whether they drink it. Readers responded to Arthur's sensationalistic narrative as if it were gospel, and the book became a bestseller. The tales of the weak-willed drunks and their hapless families grew even more popular when the book was developed into a play that ran in small towns for another half century.

Meanwhile, a group of six ex-drinkers had formed what they called the Washingtonian Total Abstinence Society. The group gathered to recount their drunken exploits, salvation through faith and abstinence, and the belief the meetings themselves could help keep them sober. The tales of down-and-out drunkenness had wide appeal as cautionary tales, and attracted crowds of men and women, northerners and southerners, laborers and educated elite.

The lurid popular fiction and stirring testimony helped galvanize a movement of middle-class women, who responded as if it were a national imperative. They crafted an absolutist message: All drinking, any drinking, could bring with it only disaster. In 1874, a group launched the Woman's Christian Temperance Union in Cleveland, Ohio.

The WCTU, which required that members be white, Protestant women born in North America, quickly spread East, where the group faced an enormous challenge: millions of new immigrants who were arriving from central and southern Europe, and whose cultures and faiths gave them a very different relationship with alcohol. Overwhelmingly Roman Catholic, Jewish, or Greek Orthodox, they drank moderately, regularly, and, shockingly, even as part of their religious celebrations.

The WCTU hoped to demonstrate the wisdom of abstinence by education and example, but it was up against some powerful traditions—centuries of moderate drinking that were accepted and tolerated by women, and encouraged even by religious leaders.

The mission, of course, was about much more than booze. The women leading the antialcohol crusade had roots in rural America and were deeply suspicious of cities, which now teemed with baffling customs. From Denver and Milwaukee to Newark and St. Louis, German-born brewers established industrial breweries that produced rivers of urban beer. German immigrant communities re-created their traditional beer gardens, which entire families attended—even on Sundays. In New York, Boston, and Philadelphia, Jewish, Italian, and Greek women not only drank wine at the dinner table, they also served small amounts to their kids.

Still more shocking, many of these new female arrivals left their homes every day for long hours in garment and textile factories. The WTCU disapproved, failing to note that the women were motivated by poverty—not a lack of education about the importance of domestic virtue. To combat this great ignorance, the group set up shop on Ellis Island, so they could indoctrinate women in the righteous ways of their new land as soon as their papers were processed.

If the WCTU failed to impress immigrant mothers, the group had a second chance through their children. The group dispatched its deputies—young teachers—into schools. Under pressure from dry lobbyists, Congress had mandated that a quarter of all health and hygiene lessons include temperance education, and the approved texts left no room for doubt. In one, a boy drops dead a few hours after he takes a nip from a flask; another described how alcohol burst blood vessels. One warned how booze transformed the robust muscles of the heart into pure fat, "sometimes so soft that a finger could be pushed through its walls."

Young schoolmarms—by the late nineteenth century teaching was an almost all-female profession—were also instructed to persuade students to sign pledges of total abstinence, or T.A. (from this derived the term "teetotaler"). Imagine the confusion of immigrant children, learning by day of alcohol's deathly properties, yet watching their parents sip beer at night.

To members of the WCTU, alcohol was the common thread in all social ills, from poverty, prostitution, and domestic violence to urban overcrowding—even women in the workplace. (If men didn't drink, the argument went, their wives wouldn't need to work.) A ban on the manufacture and sale of alcohol was the only possible solution.

Without the vote, temperance leaders could never achieve it. So they forged an alliance with early suffragists. Two of the most prominent, Elizabeth Cady Stanton and Susan B. Anthony, had joined the temperance movement early, and it was through their involvement in the antialcohol campaign that they helped gain credibility for the women's vote. It was an awkward partnership. To many middle-class Americans, the suffragists, absent temperance, seemed radical and unladylike. But the WCTU, with its symbol of purity—a tidy white ribbon—was an acceptable cause into which women could channel their ambitions.

By the early 1900s, temperance groups had branches in every state, and had adopted increasingly aggressive tactics. Activists, mostly women, surrounded saloons to sing hymns, hoping their prayers would convert the men inside. (Saloon owners often responded by "baptizing" the women with buckets of beer tossed their way.) The reformers made unannounced "shaming" visits to the homes of women they suspected of making "too free use" of alcohol. And some were masters of publicity. Carry Nation, a manic middle-aged Kentuckian, traversed the Southeast with an axe, smashing whiskey barrels and barrooms in what she called divinely inspired "hatchetations." She said her activism stemmed from her first marriage to an abusive heavy drinker whom she blamed for their daughter's poor health. Arrested for vandalism more than thirty times, she paid for her jail fines with speaking fees and the sale of souvenir hatchets. Part vaudeville, all mad, Nation inveighed against "Demon Rum," describing herself as a "bulldog running along the feet of Jesus, barking at what He doesn't like."

I wanted to get beyond the hyperbole of the reformers, and found the work of Madelon Powers, a lively professor at the University of New Orleans who has devoted most of her career to the study of urban working-class customs.

On a frigid December day, Powers was visiting New York from Louisiana and we met at her hotel in the Lower East Side. We planned to take a neighborhood walking tour in which Powers would point out former saloons and speakeasies, but the wind was bitter, so we got into my car instead. At lunch, we ducked into McSorley's Ale House, which has been in operation since the 1850s and still has a layer of sawdust on the floor. Before Prohibition, saloon keepers coated their floors every morning with a fresh layer of sawdust or wood chips, which absorbed spilled beer and urine, was easy to sweep, and masked the stink of the combined fluids.

Over hearty chicken soup and the roar of some firefighters celebrating behind us, Powers described her decades of research into business records, letters, music, photographs, and diaries. The saloon, she says, was the central feature in the lives of the urban working class: a meeting place, a reminder of the old country, and a crucial spot for the organizing of both unions and social clubs. Perhaps most important, in pre-Prohibition industrial America, the saloon was where much of the urban labor force ate their midday meals. For the cost of a nickel beer, they received a hot lunch. Amid the slog of factory work, the lunches refreshed and revived. "It drove the reformers crazy, because they lured female customers, too," she says.

Powers recounts the story of a Mrs. Mooney, an Irish laundress in New York who was outraged when a young coworker collapsed from exhaustion. It's "them rotten cold lunches you girls eat," Mrs. Mooney declared, and marched the women to a nearby saloon for a hot lunch. "Six beers with the trimmins!" Mrs. Mooney ordered, to the shock of one young colleague, Dorothy Richardson. "I, who never before could endure the sight or smell of beer, found myself draining my 'schooner' as eagerly as Mrs. Mooney herself," Richardson said later. "I instantly determined never again to blame a working man or woman for dining in a saloon in preference to the more godly and respectable dairy-lunch room."

Mrs. Mooney and Miss Richardson were by no means the exception. Powers found that a great number of respectable female drinkers frequented saloons through the discreet "ladies' entrance," commonly placed in the side or rear of the building. This allowed them to avoid public scrutiny; to bypass such indelicate barroom features as urinal troughs, positioned right beneath the bar; and to have easy access to the "take-out" counter where many women (or their children) came for large buckets of beer called "growlers." Seldom, Powers says, were they prostitutes.

But the image of ordinary women enjoying drinks in the saloon—or their take-out beer buckets on their roofs, porches, and courtyards—is mostly lost to history. "Theirs," she says, "wasn't the story the country cared about."

Instead, she says, the nation worked itself into a frenzy over lunchtime beer. Certainly, alcohol sometimes resulted in domestic violence, and of course some men drank their wages away. But many such stories were exaggerated for political effect, and lurid tales like Arthur's *Ten Nights* were told—and retold—with evangelical zeal. Alcohol consumption had declined considerably since it was at its peak in the 1820s, aided not only by clean drinking water but also by America's other emerging beverage, coffee. By the late nineteenth century, its mass-scale production in South America had made it affordable, and the invention of the percolator simplified preparation.

•   •   •

By the early 1900s, several states and many counties prohibited the sale and consumption of alcohol. The stated goal, in part, was to prove how "truly American" their populations were. The WCTU, together with the efforts of the Anti-Saloon League, which formed as a lobbying group, were also buoyed by anti-German sentiment in the years leading up to World War I. Rejecting the beer made by German immigrants, suspected of being loyal to the Kaiser, could help demonstrate one's patriotism.

Abstaining from alcohol didn't mean middle-class women refused all mood-altering substances: They were principal users of opiates, which were available over the counter and by mail order. In 1897, the Sears, Roebuck catalogue offered a kit with a syringe, two needles, two vials of heroin, and a handy carrying case for $1.50.

They also made Lydia Pinkham a wealthy woman. Pinkham marketed an herbal tonic for ailments from cramps to menopause. Pinkham was a temperance supporter, but 20 percent of her herbal tonic was alcohol. She said it was used as a "preservative."

Not even all temperance reformers were actually "dry." Many Victorian-era women, including reformers, indulged in dainty drinking rituals of their own. It was hardly even *drinking* to sip sherry or Madeira with guests, or enjoy a cool gin and tonic after a tiring day shopping. In any case, ladies knew their limits. And if they didn't, women's magazines instructed the untutored just how much liquor to pour to achieve "gaiety" but avoid getting sloshed. It was unchecked *male* drinking — the kind that took place without female supervision — that had to be stopped.

In 1919, after decades of vandalized saloons and public protests, the antialcohol forces triumphed, pushing through a constitutional amendment banning the manufacture, distribution, and sale of beer, wine, and spirits in all forty-eight states.

•   •   •

Women enthusiastically joined the millions of Americans who flouted the new law, which took effect in January 1920. Many of those who did were among the small but growing number of women who had stepped into the male world — of universities, employment, even the battlefield. And once they arrived, they had no intention of returning to the narrow world of their mothers. Twenty-one thousand American women had served as nurses during World War I, exposed to fear, death — and gallons of French wine. Tens of thousands more had attended college. Fewer than 10 percent of Americans sought higher education in 1920, but if they did, they found a near-equal ratio of male and female students. It was so common for women to join the booze-fueled socializing there that it inspired a popular joke: "She doesn't drink / She doesn't pet / She hasn't been to college yet."

Many young women also worked before they married. They took jobs in offices and department stores; in publishing, real estate, and hospitals. By the end of the decade the workforce was almost a quarter female, up from 15 percent in 1890. Women had the vote, some made their own money, and they often lived on their own in small apartments or girls' dorms. Vacuum cleaners, electric washers, and plug-in irons had eased the drudgery of housework. Even preparing food was easier: There were cold cuts from the deli, canned vegetables, and ready-sliced bread from the corner store.

All this gave young women something their forebears could never have imagined: leisure time. Untethered to a family, these new women helped fuel a culture that revolved around consumer goods and mass entertainment—around fun. They wore short dresses, tossing their restrictive corsets and knee-length bloomers for step-in panties. They bobbed their hair, smoked cigarettes, swore, painted their faces, and even experimented with sex. In *This Side of Paradise*, F. Scott Fitzgerald shocked readers with his portrayal of the debutante Rosalind, who declares that she has kissed dozens of men, and would probably kiss "dozens more." To Victorian sensibilities, such words were downright pornographic: Respectable girls were to kiss only the man they intended to marry.

It was this very group of people—the educated middle and upper-middle classes—that set the standards of national behavior. And among them, defiance of Prohibition quickly became the social norm. These new women were nobody's moral guardian: They were tomboy drinking buddies. "Women who, a few years before, would have blanched at the idea that they would ever be 'under the influence of alcohol' found themselves matching the men drink for drink," wrote essayist Frederick Lewis Allen. "They, too," he wrote, enjoyed its "uproarious release."

*   *   *

By the early 1930s, it was clear the Prohibition experiment had failed. Instead of disappearing, alcohol generated enormous profits for organized crime and crooked politicians. Illicitly manufactured alcohol had blinded, paralyzed, and killed scores of Americans. Even many female reformers, dismayed at the results of the ban, threw their efforts behind repeal.

After the stock market crashed, business leaders argued that the taxing of legal alcohol sales would raise much-needed revenues. And rebooting America's breweries and distilleries (wine would come a few years later) would help put the 25 percent of unemployed Americans back to work.

On December 5, 1933, Congress voted to repeal the Eighteenth Amendment. It had the desired effect on the government's dire fiscal straits. In the first year, consumption was estimated at one gallon per person, and alcohol sales yielded $259 million in federal taxes.

But Prohibition had lasting cultural effects, especially on women. The slamming of the saloon doors gave rise to an exciting, coed culture of drinking. In countless towns and cities, speakeasies were a force for social change, mixing men and women, blacks and whites (at least in the North). It also gave rise to a new form of entertainment: jazz.

It spurred some practical changes. One was table service, since not even a prostitute could holler her order at the bar. The second, mercifully, was the powder room, since in mixed company men couldn't relieve themselves in floor troughs. Ladies Night was decades away, but it was a start.

Prohibition also changed the way Americans drank. In speakeasies, the focus was on liquor—or, as the code of the day put it, "seeing a man about a dog." Patrons drank, and drank quickly, so they could accomplish their goal before it was time to leave (or before the feds showed up). Evening cruises, popular in coastal cities, had the same effect. These "ships to nowhere" sailed into international waters, served copious amounts of alcohol, and returned their inebriated passengers to shore. Like the frat parties that would come decades later, these developments normalized public drunkenness.

Prohibition also fundamentally changed drinking habits at home. As historian Catherine Gilbert Murdock put it, the Eighteenth Amendment "let domestic drinking out of the closet." In speakeasies, the presence of women took male drinking behavior down a notch, with fewer brawls, more flirting. At home, the opposite occurred. Sipping claret in the dining room was just as illegal as guzzling bathtub gin at a bar. So even at home, drinking took on an urgency, in back rooms and damp basements. Dainty Victorian drinking rituals, so decidedly old-fashioned, belonged to the past—and stayed there.

Ironically, the temperance reformers, in demanding a national abstinence to be overseen by the moral authority of women, created instead an irresistible underground for female drinkers. And despite the passage of almost a century, it is where many women still reside: secretly, drinking to get drunk, hiding the evidence before the authorities—their husbands, their neighbors, their kids—find out.

●　　●　　●

The reformers' image of the drinker as morally bankrupt persisted, of course, but after Prohibition ended, it attached itself mainly to women who drank. Since legislating integrity hadn't cured the nation of its habit, society had to consider other ways of looking at drinkers—at least male ones. In the nascent field of alcohol studies, there was a growing theory that liquor created a physical and psychological dependence. Men who fell prey to its powers were not so much weak as they were ill, and deserving of compassion.

This belief did not extend to women. Women who drank too much weren't just inferior—they were sideshow freaks. They were so far outside the margins, they barely merited mention even in the new medical field. By midcentury, the most notable work involving women and alcohol was a sturdy-looking book called *The Alcoholic Woman: Case Studies in the Psychodynamics of Alcoholism.*

The author, Benjamin Karpman, had an impressive résumé: He was a professor of psychiatry at Howard University College of Medicine, a member of the New York Academy of Sciences, and for decades the chief medical officer at St. Elizabeth's, a preeminent psychiatric hospital in Washington, D.C.

His 1948 book on women and alcohol established him as an authority on the subject, even though his writing merely reflected the conventional opinions of the day. Karpman laid out his jaundiced view of female drinkers in his preface, writing: "What alcoholic women seem to lack in quantity, they certainly make up in quality. . . . [A]lcoholic women are much more abnormal than alcoholic men; in common parlance, when an alcoholic woman goes on a tear, 'it is terrific.'"

In 1934, Karpman was asked to give a talk about female alcoholics to fellow psychiatrists. Though he confessed to knowing little about the subject, the address nevertheless created a considerable stir, with articles in the national press, followed by requests for help from desperate strangers. Karpman then decided to profile three female inpatients who drank to excess. Their stories, he wrote, were intended to represent "a *certain* type of alcoholic woman" (the italics are his). "It need not be thought, however, that *all* alcoholic women are as difficult and are as promiscuous sexually or lead a checkered sex life." He added this reassuring coda for worried husbands: "I have had under my care cases of alcoholic women who were very chaste and entirely faithful to their spouses."

But those stories didn't merit telling. Instead, it was the morally dubious pasts of his three patients that *seemed* right, since their experiences mirrored what people expected of female drinkers. Women, he said simply, were "more difficult to cure than alcoholic men partly because theirs are more complex problems and partly because it is hard to keep them in treatment."

He attributed the excess drinking of a patient named Frances to her subconscious desire for women: Liquor allowed her to "escape" when she had to endure "normal" intercourse with her husband.

Another patient, Vera, had a sadistic mother who lamented that Vera had survived the childhood illnesses that had killed her brothers. "Why couldn't it have been you?" she would cry as she beat the girl. Karpman made no comment on the mother's cruelty, or the serial loss and violence that marked Vera's young life. Instead, he described her as a knowing, naughty nymphet. At age fourteen, he asserted, she was "seduced" by a thirty-year-old coworker of her mother's from whom she contracted gonorrhea; other sexual partners followed. (If Karpman had any judgment on a man who sought sex with a child, he withheld it.)

Vera longed to go to the movies or out for ice cream with her friends, but since her mother disapproved of such trifles, she had no way to pay for them. One day, an elderly man approached her on the school grounds, offering her a dollar for each time she would fondle him. She agreed, thinking ahead to the freedom spending money might bring her. Karpman seized on this as evidence of her depravity: Vera was a prostitute! Once, she snatched a ten-dollar bill from the old man's hands, an infraction he reported—and that landed Vera in reform school. Karpman did not question this injustice, or the motives of the pervert, whom he described as "an eccentric old man": it was Vera who was the sexual degenerate. Her drinking was added proof of it.

The third woman, Elizabeth, also had physically and emotionally abusive parents. The insecure Elizabeth sought reassurance through sex, but could only achieve orgasm through masturbation or (gasp!) oral sex. She was, he wrote, "most unattractive" and a "general flop"—divorced, childless, and suffered from a penis envy so severe she had to drink herself to numb the pain of it. But her real debauchery came in what she said was a history of forced intercourse. Karpman scoffed at this. "Rape," he wrote, "was her specialty."

Karpman evinced no sympathy for his patients, or so much as a shred of compassion for the broken childhoods, the lost siblings, the physical abuse, or the sexual violence they suffered. By the mid–twentieth century, psychoanalysts had gained wide acceptance for their theories on a wide range of behaviors, and Karpman was a nationally respected expert. Like his colleague Bruno Bettelheim, who held mothers liable for their children's autism, Karpman blamed his patients' drinking on their licentiousness and their inability to accept their roles as wives and mothers.

Colleagues revered Karpman, the author of dozens of academic studies, as an unparalleled thinker. So did the lay press, from *Time* to *Playboy*, which quoted him frequently on sexually charged topics. In an obituary, a protégé remembered him as a "dedicated champion of the dispossessed." But when it came to women who drank too much, Karpman merely added a scientific veneer to conventional wisdom—and a national anxiety about the postwar role of women.

After two decades of tumult—first with the Depression, then the war—men and women had undergone significant shifts. Women had gained economic importance within their families by producing their own goods and stepping up to fill jobs even in heavy industry, showing their ample ability to assume male roles. But once the war was over, social critics were dismayed by anything less than a return to separate spheres. That included a national obsession with where—and how—women drank.

A New York columnist described the "Bistro Berthas, Cocktail Lounge Lorettas and Barfly Beatrices" as "1947's Problem People." Such behavior, he wrote, was "sickening to people who respect womanhood and think that women's place, while it may no longer be strictly in the home, is certainly not in the corner dive." *Newsweek* had a name for these women: "Mrs. Drunkard."

Noel Busch, a writer at *Life* magazine, issued a stern reprimand in 1947. "In the olden days lady tipplers were rare to start with, and what few there were at least tried to conceal their weakness, shut up in some attic and ignored by society. Of late, however, they have entered into the broad daylight." He blamed the trend on women's efforts to achieve parity, which had "merely gotten them more mixed up than they were in the first place." He admonished them to "go back to cooking, sweeping, and attending to their children." He was aghast that women should enter bars—which, after all, were "men's clubs—not a hospital for housewives with the fidgets." They should order wine or beer—nothing that would take the barkeep's time—and after thirty minutes, get up and go home. "Drinking in the home, of course, poses other questions—but at least does not constitute a public menace." Of the dozen or so ads the issue carried for beer and whiskey, not a single one showed a woman.

Through it all, Karpman's *Alcoholic Woman* remained riveting enough to sustain readers' interests. It went through several printings in the 1950s, was released as a mass-market paperback in 1966, and was published continuously until 1974. Karpman's voice, likewise, was that of an expert—*the* expert—on troubled female drinkers, and what was perceived as their twisted desires, for almost a quarter century.

4 *One Day at a Time:*
A.A. and Women

If a woman had an uncontrollable drinking problem, there were few places she could turn. By the late 1940s, Alcoholics Anonymous had taken root as the nation's most popular remedy for excess drinking. Founded by two men in the mid-1930s, A.A. was initially inhospitable to women. Early members told women who were daring—or desperate—enough to attend its meetings that female alcoholics simply didn't exist. Nice ones, anyway.

The story of A.A.'s beginnings and its cofounder Bill Wilson has been told many times, first by Wilson himself and later, often from the affectionate perspective of writers who felt they or their loved ones had benefited from the program. In barest terms, the tale is this: Wilson and a small group of men created a fellowship of laymen whose personal experi-

ences helped other sufferers triumph over a malady that re-
sisted all other remedies. Most of the early members were
upper-middle-class men like Wilson—lawyers, stockbrokers,
and other professionals brought low by alcohol.

I scoured the literature for clues about the role of women.
In its early days, there wasn't much, but what little I could
find suggested that the group took a dim view of female talents
and possibilities—and was intolerant of their flaws. Historians suggest that these attitudes should be understood in the
context of the period. But as I looked at A.A.'s treatment of
women in the modern era, I found numerous echoes of the
past. History casts a long shadow within A.A., a group that
venerates its founders and whose members can quote sections
of Wilson's 1939 text, known as the Big Book, by heart.

Today, A.A.'s approach to alcoholism has come to domi-
nate alcohol treatment in the United States. If you seek professional help, the odds are overwhelming that you will be
referred to a program that is founded on the notion that problem drinkers are powerless in the face of a disease and must
religiously follow twelve steps if they hope to stay sober. If
you get arrested for driving while drunk, or admit to a court
that alcohol was involved in a crime, there's a good chance
you'll be ordered to attend A.A. meetings, sometimes by a
judge who's been through the program. In more than 90 percent of the nation's rehab facilities, the twelve steps of A.A.
are the foundation of treatment. Its popularity, I discovered,
was more a matter of historical happenstance than scientific
choice. A.A. has legions of supporters and devoted, grateful
followers, and its twelve-step model for recovery has been
replicated in myriad ways in American culture.

But there are many other evidence-based approaches that

researchers say are superior to the faith-based model. There is also a growing chorus of addiction experts who suggest that its key tenet—that problem drinkers are powerless over drink— might actually undermine women's efforts to get well. It is worth noting that no other industrialized country relies on this approach for treating people with alcohol problems to the extent the United States does. The commitment to twelve-step programs is as American as baseball and big-budget disaster movies. To understand how we got here, you need to journey back to the Great Depression.

In the 1930s, Bill Wilson was an unsuccessful stockbroker and a "chronic inebriate" who had drunk his way through Prohibition. Desperate to stop, he sought the help of a friend who had found sobriety through the evangelical Oxford Group. It believed that men were sinners who, through confession and God's help, could right their paths and help others.

Wilson was intrigued, but he still couldn't quit drinking, and in 1934 he checked into Manhattan's Towns Hospital for his fourth attempt at drying out. There, his doctor, William Silkworth, told him that his condition was the result of an illness—not a moral shortcoming. Over a four-day period, Silkworth gave Wilson a powerful cocktail that included the hallucinogen belladonna, sedatives, and laxatives. The hope of the treatment, seen as a last resort, was that after several days of vomiting and diarrhea, the hallucinogen could psychically jolt drunks into sobriety. Patients called the method, which had been developed by a life insurance salesman named Charles Towns, "purge and puke."

It worked for Wilson. Lying in his hospital bed, Wilson shouted out to God to reveal himself. He then reported seeing a blinding light and feeling the most serene calm he had ever experienced. He left the hospital, joined the Oxford Group, and stopped drinking for good. In 1935, on a business trip to Akron, Ohio, Wilson contacted another Oxford Group member, a proctologist named Bob Smith.

Together, they formed Alcoholics Anonymous, based loosely on the Oxford Group philosophies, the Washingtonians' nineteenth-century group meetings, and Benjamin Rush's eighteenth-century concept that excessive drinking was a sickness. By coming together for mutual support and spirituality, alcoholics could help each other keep from drinking, one day at a time. Though they made exceptions for themselves, the founders agreed that members should be anonymous. It was as much a defense against individual self-importance and stigma as it was a protection for the group. (They reasoned that the failures of any well-known members would embarrass the organization.) While they didn't advocate abstention for everybody, Wilson and Smith were unequivocal: For problem drinkers like themselves, one drop of booze was like a match tossed into a pool of gasoline.

Wilson and Smith developed the now-famous twelve steps. At their core was a declaration of powerlessness over alcohol. Members were encouraged to admit that their thirst for booze was beyond their control. To regain their health, excessive drinkers needed to relinquish their self-centeredness and submit to a higher power. Eventually, they could regain their footing and help other drunks do the same. There was little else in the way of hope for alcoholics, and by the late 1930s the group spread to a few dozen men in the Midwest and New York, eventually attracting a handful of women.

Like many innovators, Wilson was complicated, and once he stopped drinking, his other, equally ravenous appetites became apparent. He downed astonishing quantities of coffee, chain-smoked the cigarettes that would ultimately kill him, and was a compulsive womanizer. He suffered from deep depressions, which many of his friends believed were triggered by the guilt he felt about repeatedly betraying his wife, Lois. Eventually, he became an enthusiast of LSD, for both himself and other alcoholics; at the time, science was intrigued by its potential as a tool for a variety of psychiatric conditions. He took megadoses of niacin as a mood regulator, and developed a passion for conducting séances in his home in Westchester County, New York, where he claimed to receive frequent messages "from the other side."

His philandering was an open secret. In the 1960s, longtime A.A.s became so alarmed by his constant attraction to young female newcomers, they formed what they called "Founder's Watch," a group of friends delegated to steer Bill away from pretty women who caught his eye during A.A. functions. For the last fifteen years of his life, Wilson had an affair with an A.A. colleague and beautiful actress twenty-two years his junior, Helen Wynn. Unlike Lois, who was a normal drinker, downing a single cocktail before dinner every night, Wynn was a recovering alcoholic who followed the A.A. program. Though he could not know it, the early tolerance for Bill's sexual conduct would set a behavioral precedent for the organization.

As the group spread, Wilson and other early members drew up a blueprint they titled *Alcoholics Anonymous: The Story of How More Than One Hundred Men Have Recovered from Alcoholism.*

It was, in effect, a New Deal for drunks—as long as the drunks were men. Women were barely mentioned. Near the end of the first edition of *Alcoholics Anonymous,* the unnamed author—though the book was a joint project, Wilson is said to have been its chief writer—concedes that the program could help women, too. But in the A.A. worldview, a woman's most conceivable role was as the wife of an alcoholic. In a chapter called "To Wives," the text offers women specific instructions for bolstering their husbands' precarious mental health. Never be angry, the book warns, even if you have to leave your husband temporarily. "Patience and good temper are most necessary.... If he gets the idea that you are a nag or a killjoy, your chance of accomplishing anything useful may be zero.... He will tell you he is misunderstood. This may lead to lonely evenings for you." Wilson hinted at the unpleasant consequences for wives who didn't take his advice: "He may seek someone else to console him—not always another man."

The book included a brief chapter written by the group's second female member, a divorced housewife named Florence R. The self-loathing she felt at being a filly in a stable of stallions is painfully apparent. "To my lot falls the rather doubtful distinction of being the only 'lady' alcoholic in our particular section," she wrote. "I have learned to recognize and acknowledge the underlying cause of my disease: selfishness, self-pity, and resentment." A few months later, Florence R. (later identified as Florence Rankin) resumed drinking and committed suicide.

The book made clear that men who drank too much were in the grips of a disease that gave them an uncontrollable urge. In the view of A.A. members and others, women drinkers had themselves to blame. They were widely seen as trollops, their drinking a symptom of unchecked libidos. Records from the period show the men of A.A. worried about what might hap-

pen if these femmes fatales mixed with male sufferers, sometimes with good reason. In A.A.'s early days, a former Akron
mayor consummated his affair with a woman on Dr. Bob's ex-
amining table. The episode scandalized the group. "As drunks,
I don't know why we should have been," Bill would later say,
adding that the woman was the first they had ever dealt with.
In any case, the incident left the impression that women could
bring only one thing: trouble. Bill and others feared such antics would disrupt the organization entirely.

Male drinkers often had the support of intact families,
even if only because their wives were financially dependent
on them. But few men tolerated alcoholic women, and many
of the first female A.A.s were divorced or single—and therefore posed a threat to the wives. Men developed a truism of
their own: "Under every skirt there is a slip." Dalliances with
women trying to get sober were sure to provoke a relapse.

To manage this potential distraction, women who did come
sat opposite men in the rooms. And women were sponsored
not by other alcoholics, but by the alcoholics' wives. Eventually, the group developed "closed" and "open" meetings,
which anyone was welcome to attend. Women-only meetings
developed, too—but those quickly generated controversy, as
the women who attended were suspected of being lesbians.

There was a woman among the founders of A.A., and she
played a crucial role in popularizing the group. Her name was
Marty Mann, and in 1939, she was in a Connecticut sanitarium
headed toward the same dismal fate as Florence R. Born into
a wealthy Chicago family that counted the educator Horace
Mann among its forebears, Mann was a debutante, educated
at exclusive private schools. Married and divorced by twenty-
five, she had joined the hard-drinking field of public relations

after her family lost its fortune in the 1929 crash. On a usual day, she'd have a few swigs and six martinis—and that was just before lunch. One night, so drunk she couldn't remember if she jumped or fell, Mann plunged from a second-story window in London, breaking multiple bones. She checked into the Connecticut hospital to dry out, but kept sneaking out for drinks. When her psychiatrist gave her the manuscript of the Big Book, she recoiled at its religious message, and put it away.

During a fit of anger weeks later, Mann picked up the book again. This time, she described feeling her rage lift and her hopelessness recede. She left the sanitarium and sought out A.A. in New York. Her blue-blood lineage may have helped persuade the male members she was respectable, but she was far from accepted. To the men, Mann recalled, she was "just some kind of a freak." Ironically, it was the wives who helped welcome her. Mann was a lesbian, and posed no romantic risks with the men.

With her skills in public relations, Mann quickly emerged as an effective messenger for the idea that alcoholics were sick and deserving of compassion and help. Wilson was the architect of the twelve-step program, but Mann planted A.A. in the public consciousness. Her prominence was striking among the all-male leadership, especially one so hostile to women.

Mann had three "slips" during her first eighteen months in the program, which underscored her fears of helplessness—and helped fuel male doubts about her participation. "Nobody thought it was possible that I, or any other woman, would ever make it," she later recalled.

It didn't stop her from reaching out to other female drinkers. She estimated that in her first year, she had tried to help at least a hundred women, but only she and three other women showed up regularly at the new New York office. "This was a man's problem and A.A. was a man's program and this was a man's world," Mann would later say. As late as 1959, Mann noted disapprovingly, many A.A. chapters continued to refuse to admit women.

She blamed the predicament on the enduring double standard that regarded male drunkenness as acceptable on some occasions—but always deplored the same behavior in women. It's no wonder, she would say, even decades after A.A.'s founding, that women went underground with their drinking. "We hide," she said. "We do our drinking in our bedroom, at least as much as we can, until we're too drunk to know the difference and we go wandering out, and everybody does find out."

The double standard, she said, was also why getting help was so hard for women. "I knew an awful lot of women the first years I was in A.A. who couldn't make it, who didn't make it," she said. "I always felt in many cases it was because they were women—not because they were so much sicker, or because they didn't want to make it, but the odds were so stacked against them that they never really had a chance." It didn't dawn on Mann, though, that perhaps the solution that had worked for her was not appropriate for other women.

Mann did not appear to have experienced any doubts. In 1944, she established a foundation called the National Committee for Education on Alcoholism (it would later become the National Council on Alcoholism). She went public with her name, contrary to the A.A.'s rules guarding anonymity, in the hope that her regal carriage and solid upbringing could show that anybody, even women, could be afflicted with the disease of alcoholism.

●   ●   ●

Paradoxically, A.A.'s remedy for this disease was a purely spiritual approach. But since doctors could only offer such dubious cures as belladonna, A.A.'s faith-based methods filled a therapeutic vacuum. Nonetheless, its founders hungered for the medical community's stamp of approval, and an after-the-fact search for scientific proof of A.A.'s efficacy for treating alcoholism was a natural next step. Science could boost the movement, and so the research, funded in part by alcohol companies, began. Those efforts, it turned out, weren't terribly rigorous, even by standards of the day. Not surprisingly, they excluded women.

The epicenter of the nascent field of alcohol research was Yale's Center for Alcohol Studies. Its researchers founded a journal, devised Yale Plan treatment clinics, and instituted a six-week summer school of alcohol studies to educate clergy, temperance workers, probation officers, and medical professionals in the revolutionary way of viewing the problem drinker. Founded in 1942, the Yale center launched a medical movement around the concept of alcoholism as a disease. Americans had dedicated countless resources to demonize the evils of alcohol, but now came a swift reversal: The nation didn't have an alcohol problem; alcoholics did.

Mann attended the Yale summer school and began to work closely with the center's top researcher, an enigmatic biostatistician named E. M. Jellinek. Mann's skills in crafting strategic communications and Jellinek's scientific mantle were mutually beneficial: Jellinek received widespread attention for his research, while Mann's ties to the prestigious institution lent her—and A.A., apprehensive that its insistence on member abstinence would link it to old-fashioned temperance groups—credibility.

Jellinek was by all accounts a polyglot and charming colleague. His qualifications, however, were dubious, and his curriculum vitae included at least one invented degree: a 1936 doctorate in science from the University of Leipzig. Jellinek was Jewish, and by that date Jews in Hitler's Germany were barred from sitting for their doctorates.

Jellinek's scientific rigor was equally questionable. Data for one of his early studies, on the psychological and physical trajectory of alcoholism, came from questionnaires devised not by Yale researchers but by A.A.'s General Service Office (GSO) in New York. Of the 1,600 questionnaires mailed, only 158 people responded. Working together, Mann and Jellinek tossed the forty-five that were incomplete or indecipherable, and another fifteen that had come from women. Their answers diverged so far from the men's that they would have changed the findings. So the physiologist and the PR lady, keen to promote the disease theory—each for their own reasons—decided to discard them.

This left ninety-eight self-selected white men, not exactly a scientifically representative sample. From them, Jellinek published a 1946 paper that was seminal in the establishment of alcoholism as a disease. Using the answers on the questionnaires, he came up with a theory of how people succumb to alcohol, in a series of stages that closely replicated the A.A. experience. Over the next many years, it came to be illustrated by a curve in which alcoholics progressed from normal social drinking to sneaking drinks, then to increased tolerance, guilt, blackouts, withdrawal symptoms, and hopelessness, then finally to a low point where the drinker realizes he must reform. The chart circulated nationwide.

Jellinek continued to refine his theories in the years that followed, and as he did, he began to distance himself from much of the popular interpretations of his work. He became especially concerned about the widespread use of the word "alcoholic." As he rightly noted, everybody from social scientists to journalists and general practitioners had adopted it as the label for any kind of excess drinking—not only the distinct, well-defined behaviors that eventually led to physical dependence. The misapplication of the word could only undermine the whole disease concept, he warned in 1952: If everybody could attribute bad drunken behavior to a disease, they couldn't possibly be accountable for it.

In his 1960 book, *The Disease Concept of Alcoholism,* Jellinek described five "phases" of alcoholism he arbitrarily identified with Greek letters. "Gamma" alcoholics were those who were physically and psychologically dependent—the truly diseased.

Yet Jellinek had become uncomfortable with the growing role laymen were taking in defining the affliction—and how best to treat it. He acknowledged that his conclusions were drawn from a small number of subjects, and urged the "student of alcoholism" to "emancipate himself from accepting the exclusiveness of the picture of alcoholism as propounded by Alcoholics Anonymous." At a 1959 alcoholism conference at Columbia University, he even pleaded that "A.A. leave science alone—so that scientists might get along with the business of objective research into the problem."

But that didn't happen. With his 1960 book, the press seized upon the idea that alcoholics—"real" alcoholics—had no choice about their drinking, sharing an inability to stop once they'd had a single sip. Jellinek wrote that "recovered alcoholics in Alcoholics Anonymous speak of 'loss of control' . . . when the ingestion of one alcoholic drink sets up a chain reaction so that they are unable to adhere to their intention 'to have one or two drinks only' but continue to ingest more and more . . . contrary to their volition."

The qualifiers—"recovered alcoholics in Alcoholics Anonymous"—were overlooked. Like the fictional ten nights in a barroom that galvanized the temperance workers, Jellinek's findings seeped into the public consciousness as scientific fact.

As someone who has written for various daily publications for more than twenty years, I can understand the impulse to emphasize the most dramatic findings under deadline pressure, but the effects can be damaging—and lasting. That's how we wound up with "crack babies," infants born to mothers who used that drug during pregnancy and who experts erroneously predicted would be severely mentally, physically, and emotionally disabled; and how autism got linked to vaccines (the so-called findings of Andrew Wakefield, the British doctor who first reported the connection in the *Lancet,* have been completely discredited). Unfortunately, though, many of these early (and, as it turns out, bogus) ideas take hold.

Jellinek's caveats went unnoticed, and by the time of his death in 1963, the fusing of public belief and science seemed complete. In his book *Alcohol: The World's Favorite Drug,* Griffith Edwards, a British alcohol researcher, described the climate this way: "The disease of alcoholism was the whole problem, and any other view was a heresy to be preached down. So deft and politically astute was the reformulation of the problem that it seems almost like a conjuring trick. A rabbit in the form of a disease was brought out of the hat, and alcohol vanished into thin air."

At midcentury, Americans' faith in medicine seemed boundless. Vaccines, steroids, and antibiotics vanquished deadly, painful ailments. Researchers discovered DNA; physicians performed open-heart surgery and organ transplants. And so, too, could medicine have an answer for the alcoholic.

Except for one thing: This new, medically approved program did not rely on anyone with medical training. These new helpers would be peers who had "hit bottom" themselves and, with the aid of a higher power, returned to sobriety. The cure for the hapless drinker, then, wound up being exactly where the United States had started: religion.

A.A. and Popular Culture

Marty Mann was remarkably gifted at spinning the bottle. Throughout her tenure, she met with—and by some accounts, collaborated with—reporters, broadcast executives, and Hollywood screenwriters whose work extolled the redemptive powers of A.A.

In the 1940s, newspapers and national magazines began to feature tales of male drunks saved by A.A. On radio and television shows, men poured out their emotional stories to living room audiences around the country. And in a sign of the mores of that time, those interviewed on television wore Lone Ranger masks to hide their identities.

In 1945, moviegoers turned *The Lost Weekend* into a blockbuster. The dark, edgy film, directed by Billy Wilder, was a dramatic departure from the 1930s romps of W. C.

Fields or *The Thin Man* team of Myrna Loy and William Powell, in which drinking was a comedic prop. *The Lost Weekend,* adapted from an autobiographical novel by A.A. member Charles Jackson, depicts a struggling writer who lurches through a five-day bender of shameful flashbacks and terrifying hallucinations. "He's a sick person," his girlfriend confides at a key point. "It's as though there was something wrong with his heart or his lungs. You wouldn't walk out on him if he had an attack. He needs our help."

Such compassionate language—which echoed through popular culture—went a long way in helping Americans accept that male alcoholics shared an affliction.

An orthodoxy took hold. When heavy drinkers appeared in plays, in films, and on living room television screens, the plot followed predictable lines: the drunk falls off the deep end if he or she doesn't join A.A. Singer Lillian Roth told of her descent into booze and recovery through A.A. in the worldwide best-seller, translated into twenty languages, called *I'll Cry Tomorrow.* Actress Susan Hayward earned an Oscar nomination for playing Roth in the hit movie.

By contrast, Kirsten Arneson, the alcoholic played by Lee Remick in *The Days of Wine and Roses,* rejects A.A.—and with it, all respectability. Her husband, played by Jack Lemmon, sobers up, but Kirsten doesn't, and becomes a derelict wife and mother. She even picks up strangers in bars—she prefers their company to her husband's "holier-than-thou, do-gooder Boy Scout" A.A. buddies. At the end of the film—equal parts horror movie and cautionary tale—she tells her husband, "You better give up on me."

She turns away, toward a neon bar sign glowing in the distance. Director Blake Edwards later said he had quit drinking before shooting the film. "I was one of those lucky people who found the power to stop on my own," he told the *New York Times*. Kirsten, poor unfortunate, was hopeless. She didn't fit into A.A.—but paradoxically, she was doomed without it.

The real world was hardly more empathetic to women who drank too much. Male alcoholics were celebrated for seeking A.A.'s help, but women were castigated for needing it. A Boston newspaper used the headline "Women Drunkards, Pitiful Creatures, Get Helping Hand," to describe female members of the group.

By then, A.A. began to accept greater numbers of women, but they remained decidedly second-class citizens. In 1946, the *Grapevine*, the group's monthly newsletter, printed a front-page litany of complaints about women's behavior in A.A., amassed from groups around the country. Its author was a woman, Grace O. (She noted, writing in the third person, that she was "grateful" for the anonymity that allowed her to "stick her neck out.")

She called it "Female Frailties":

1. The percentage of women who stay with A.A. is low—too many drop out after the novelty wears off.

2. Women form emotional attachments that are too intense.

3. So many women want to run things. To boss, manage, supervise, regulate, and change things. Twenty want to decorate; one will scrub or mend what is already around.

4. Too many women don't like women.

5. Women talk too much. Women . . . worry the same dead mouse until it's unrecognizable.

6. Women shouldn't work with men, and vice versa.

7. Sooner or later, a woman-on-the-make sallies into a group, on the prowl for phone numbers and dates.

8. A lot of women are attention demanders. Spotlight sisters. They want to be spoon-fed, coaxed, babied, encouraged, teased, praised, and personally conducted into recovery.

9. Few women can think in the abstract.

10. Women's feelings get hurt too often.

11. Far too many women A.A.'s cannot get along with the non-alcoholic wives of A.A. members.

These beliefs reflected an organizational opinion, as their prominent display indicated. They also revealed a deeper truth about the predicament of the woman who drank too much: It was vulgar to drink like a man, but you'd better sober up like one. Strong. Silent. Undemanding. "Spotlight sisters" who wanted to be "personally conducted into recovery" need not apply.

A.A.'s most prominent initiative for women was Al-Anon family groups. Created by Lois Wilson and Dr. Bob's spouse, Anne Smith, Al-Anon was a twelve-step program for wives of alcoholics. The organization, which would develop the theory of "codependence"—being addicted to the person with the addiction—urged women to "let go and let God." It also counseled them to provide an emotionally secure atmosphere that would solidify their husbands' sobriety. Cultural historian Lori Rotskoff suggests that this ideology—the patient, accepting wife; boys-will-be-boys husband—helped rebuild the gender roles upended by the Depression and the war. A woman's job was to maintain the family morally and emotionally; a man's was to provide financially. In the study of what came to be called "the alcoholic marriage," social workers judged wives equally responsible for their husbands' drinking. "The wife of an alcoholic is not simply the object of mistreatment in a situation which she had no part in creating," one social worker wrote. Such women fit into four neat wifely categories: Controlling Catherines, Wavering Winnifreds, Punitive Pollys, and Suffering Susans.

Paradoxically, Al-Anon offered no such convenient excuses for husbands whose wives drank to excess. There were no Demanding Dicks, Raging Roberts, or Explosive Eds to blame.

•   •   •

Few people questioned how well A.A. worked—or whether there might be gender differences in the way women and men recovered. Speaking to a Canadian audience celebrating the thirtieth anniversary of the group, Mann declared that the twelve-step approach worked equally for both genders. She did not mention that she herself had recently relapsed.

"The full realization that A.A. is just as much for women, that it works just as well for women as it does for men—is a tremendously important message."

5 *Rehab Nation*

In 1970, the United States formally embraced the twelve-step approach when Congress passed the Comprehensive Alcohol Abuse and Alcoholism Prevention, Treatment, and Rehabilitation Act. The law was known as the Hughes Act for its sponsor, Iowa senator Harold Hughes, and it dedicated millions to the study, education, and treatment of alcoholism, which in 1956 had been designated an "illness" by the American Medical Association. (It stopped short of calling it a "disease.") The legislation reflected broader American enthusiasm about the possibilities of science and technology. America had won the race to space, beating the Soviet cosmonauts to the moon, and had defeated scourges from polio to smallpox. After addressing alcoholism, Congress declared war on cancer, creating fifteen cancer research centers to invent new drugs that would combat it.

The Hughes Act created a new, centralized research agency, the National Institute for Alcohol Abuse and Alcoholism (NIAAA), with authority to develop and conduct health, education, training, research, and planning programs for the prevention and treatment of alcohol abuse and alcoholism. In the years that followed, Mann's group, renamed the National Council on Alcoholism and Drug Dependence, grew fivefold. Government funding accounted for more than 75 percent of its budget.

In addition to underwriting research, the Hughes Act barred employers from discriminating against alcoholics, a seemingly simple provision that turned out to have far-reaching implications. Companies that worried about legal liability dramatically expanded their employee assistance programs, which referred employees with drug or alcohol problems to the growing number of for-profit treatment centers springing up nationwide. At the same time, major insurers recognized alcoholism as a disease and began paying for inpatient treatment at these centers, which were overwhelmingly staffed by recovering alcoholics who remained active in A.A. and used literature sold by A.A.'s publishing arm, Alcoholics Anonymous World Services, in rehab. At typical treatment centers, patients received on-site counseling combined with other therapies. Regular attendance at A.A. meetings was an essential component of a stay.

The A.A. view of alcoholism was ideally suited to the profit needs of the rehab industry: Counseling could be delivered by people whose main qualification was having recovered from "hitting bottom" through a strict adherence to the twelve steps. Instead of hiring a staff of highly paid doctors, rehab centers could rely on laymen with life experience. The counselors established a group called the National Association of Alcohol Counselors and Trainers, in order, as one of its founders said, to "make alcoholism counselor trainers look professional." He told an interviewer: "The training we taught [our new counselors] was not based on clinical skills; it was based on a community development model with emphasis on A.A."

With insurers and companies footing the bill, rehab blossomed into the multibillion-dollar industry it is today. Consider this: In 1969, the outgoing Johnson administration had budgeted $4 million nationally for community alcohol treatment programs. Hughes, a self-declared member of A.A. who was known by his colleagues as "Mr. Addiction," said the sum would be about as effective as trying to stop the floodwaters of the Mississippi with a pebble. Hughes stepped down from the Senate after a single term, and returned to Iowa, where he became an alcohol treatment entrepreneur, founding several private centers.

In 1972, the NIAAA budget was $84.6 million; by 1975, that figure was $146 million. In 1973, there were roughly 1,800 treatment facilities. By 2009, that number had jumped to more than 13,500, nearly a third run by for-profit companies. (In 2012, the NIAAA's budget was $469 million.) Much of the alcohol research supported with federal dollars focused on the twelve-step approach.

The contrast between the research on alcohol and cancer launched by the federal government in the 1970s is illuminating. Government-supported researchers have discovered hundreds of new cancer therapies over the past four decades, and there are nearly 1,000 more biopharmaceutical cancer drugs in development. Yet there are about a mere six drugs to treat alcohol

GABRIELLE GLASER

abuse; two, Antabuse and naltrexone, were on the market long before the enactment of the Hughes Act.

As more Americans entered rehab, more joined A.A. Between 1965 and 1975, A.A. membership in the United States jumped almost 130 percent, from 144,000 to 331,000. By 1968, females accounted for 22 percent of the group.

Just as they were being accepted in A.A., many American women were beginning to challenge their position and rights in society, and taking their place inside the institutions that had been dominated by men. Congress passed Title IX, and the Supreme Court guaranteed women the right to end a pregnancy. By the end of the decade, nearly half of all women were in the workforce, and for the first time, more women than men entered colleges.

Paradoxically, these advances added burdens for millions of women with families. As they entered public life and industry, women remained responsible for the majority of housework. Sociologists found that married American women in the 1960s and '70s were working an extra month of twenty-four-hour days when compared with their husbands. (Researchers tallied the total time spent by men and women on domestic chores and child care.)

Many women accepted this imbalance to maintain peace in their marriages and to fulfill their ambitions or keep their family finances afloat. Their mothers' and grandmothers' generation had managed to raise kids and keep a clean house. But as Arlie Hochschild noted in her book *The Second Shift*, these women also suffered from exhaustion, low sex drive, irritability, and some pretty serious anxiety. In national drinking surveys taken in 1967 and 1984, the number of women in their thirties who said they were regular drinkers rose by almost 9 percent. And in that seventeen-year gap, the number of women who reported binging, being unable to stop until they were drunk, and suffering professional consequences more than doubled.

There were other dramatic social changes occurring, too: As states passed no-fault divorce laws, the divorce rate began climbing, reaching an all-time high in 1981, when more than half of all marriages dissolved.

Not surprisingly, there was a lot of public hand-wringing about the state of women—including their alcohol intake. Though American women had begun to drink more since the end of the Second World War, in the 1970s there was sudden concern about the "epidemic" of female drinking. The discovery in the 1970s and '80s that alcohol had dangerous effects on fetuses (called fetal alcohol syndrome, FAS), while legitimate and alarming, escalated concerns about women's drinking as a wider social problem. A century after the founding of the WCTU, the outcry over FAS turned attention solely on female imbibers. Suddenly, there was intense focus on women's drinking habits, regardless of whether they were pregnant. And the pressures were growing: In this brave new universe of negotiating day care and custody agreements, trying to make partner while keeping a marriage together, who had time to relax? If a woman poured herself a glass or two (or three) of the culturally sanctioned wine, she could cook dinner, fold clothes, and fall asleep. This drinking wasn't social: For many women at the breaking point, it felt like first aid.

•   •   •

Shortly after the Hughes Act became law, one of Sharon Wilsnack's Harvard professors asked her to contribute to his book on the human motivations for drinking. Wilsnack recalls that day more than forty years ago with fresh disbelief. As she read through the draft, she noticed a startling omission: In nearly six hundred pages of text, there was no mention of a single female subject. Mustering her courage, Wilsnack asked her professor why women had been overlooked. Sheepish, he admitted that he had had a "huge blind spot," and encouraged Wilsnack to learn more. Wilsnack headed to the Widener Library, one of the nation's best, to immerse herself in the existing scholarly literature on women and alcohol.

Over the next several months, she combed through books, academic journals, and papers. She found hundreds of thousands of studies of alcoholism, but only six of them involved female subjects. "And they were lousy, tiny studies," Wilsnack says. Many researchers, she discovered, had even omitted the effects of alcohol on female rats. "They had either not included them in the first place, or tossed them out because their fat ratios or estrus cycle screwed up the results," she says. "Researchers were treating women just like men, even if it was clear from the outset that there were huge differences."

One Harvard study piqued her curiosity. It had enlisted males at a frat party, asking them to look at pictures and describe their emotions at certain intervals after drinking. A large majority of the men described feeling "tough," and with greater inebriation reported feeling even more confident of their physical and social powers.

Wilsnack got funding to conduct a similar study, this time using men and women. She devised two parties for Harvard students with identical lighting, music, and ambience, but at one, they were served alcohol; at the other, soft drinks. After the students were finished imbibing, researchers showed pictures and asked them to talk about their emotions. The male drinkers reported feeling more aggressive, replicating the earlier study.

It was the early 1970s—an optimistic time to be a young woman on the Harvard campus, and Wilsnack had wondered if the female drinkers might report feeling strong and capable, too. Instead, they said the opposite of what she expected: They described feeling calmer, less inhibited, and both emotionally and physically warmer than the nondrinking female subjects.

But the female alcohol drinkers reported feeling less powerful, socially and personally, than the soda-pop-drinking women. The findings took her aback. "I had some vague ideas about what I might find," Wilsnack recalls, "but that women felt less powerful when they drank—that really surprised me."

In the wider world, women were beginning to question their treatment at the hands of the largely male medical profession, particularly when it came to pregnancy, childbirth, and menopause. Not far from Wilsnack's office, the authors of *Our Bodies, Ourselves* were researching and revising the first edition of their book, which would sell 250,000 copies without any formal advertising. Alcohol and drug abuse, in part due to the Hughes Act, was also in the public consciousness, so Wilsnack's research put her in high demand with reporters, even though she was a graduate student in her early thirties with no clinical practice.

But there was still so little known about women and alcohol. Wilsnack's two published studies brought the global literature on women and alcohol to a total of fifteen papers.

Women were all but ignored by researchers studying alcohol abuse, too. By 1976, the increasingly significant NIAAA had funded 574 treatment programs; a mere 14 of them were for women. Of 384 research grants, just 16 had any relationship to women, and only five were specifically designed for studying female drinkers.

And no one even bothered to track whether women were seeking treatment for alcohol abuse. I searched government databases for female treatment admissions for some sense of the numbers in the years between 1970 and 1985, but couldn't find them anywhere. Leigh Henderson, an epidemiologist at the Substance Abuse and Mental Health Services Administration, the agency the government created in 1992, told me why. "No single national data source covers the entire period, and there are no national data prior to 1977," she wrote in an e-mail. ". . . Data on the characteristics of females in treatment who abused alcohol alone simply do not exist for that period."

In other words, nobody was even thinking to count them.

This much is clear. When women broached their worries and anxieties with family doctors (the vast majority of whom were male), they were likely to be brushed off, prescribed Valium, and labeled "troublemakers." The 1960s might have been an epoch of free love and questioning of authority, but expectations remained high for women. In sociological surveys designed to test tolerance for the shifting mores of the 1960s and '70s, Americans across all social, class, racial, and regional lines cited contempt for drunken female behavior. The antics of inebriated men, meanwhile, were viewed far less dimly.

The Hughes Act gave people with alcohol problems a place to go. And it wasn't long before the definition of who qualified for help began to broaden. "My name's Jan, and

I'm an alcoholic," came into the national lexicon as short-hand for a lifelong condition, a course from which you could never graduate. If you could recognize yourself on Jellinek's curve, then you, too, could find a place for yourself within the A.A. narrative. Whether you thought about drinking too much; whether, during a period of stress, you looked forward to an evening cocktail too much; or whether you had progressed to the point where you had a shot of whiskey in the morning to calm the shakes, there was a cure: cold turkey and group support. It would require vigilance: At any moment, a drop of alcohol could sweep aside decades of sobriety and develop into a binge. The triggers could be as innocent as a bite of Grandma's bourbon-soaked Christmas cake, or filet mignon with red wine sauce. Some argued that even pain medication after surgery—Bill W. called them "goofballs"—could set off a bender.

While the treatment centers broadcast this gospel to a much wider audience, a handful of U.S. researchers began to question whether abstinence was an appropriate approach for everyone with worrisome drinking habits. In 1976, the Rand Corporation released results of a study of more than two thousand subjects—all male—who were patients at forty-five NIAAA-funded treatment centers. The report, underwritten by NIAAA, analyzed a wide range of data about the patients, but a small passage in the findings generated a huge controversy. Researchers found that eighteen months after alcohol treatment, 24 percent of the men were abstaining, and another 22 percent were drinking moderately, reporting no associated problems. The authors concluded that it was possible for some alcohol-dependent men to return to controlled drinking.

Separately, two California researchers, Mark and Linda

Sobell, reported success with teaching alcohol-dependent subjects to drink in moderation using behavior modification. All of the Sobells' seventy subjects were male.

You would have thought the scientists had reported that a steady diet of bacon grease was good for your heart. Attacks from some researchers at Marty Mann's organization, the National Council on Alcoholism, were swift and vitriolic, and charged that the news would lead alcoholics to falsely believe they could drink safely. Prominent NCA board members tried to suppress the findings drawn from the treatment center data, and the NIAAA, which had funded the study, repudiated it. In response to the criticism, Rand researchers expanded their study to include more subjects, this time for a four-year period, with similar results—and equally fevered reactions. The second study included 922 subjects, all men. The Sobells fared little better. They were accused of fraud, ridiculed in the scientific and popular media, and ultimately moved to Canada, where they replicated their findings without causing a furor.

The root of the angry responses was obvious to many researchers, especially the late Alan Marlatt, a psychologist at the University of Washington who defended the experiments in follow-up journal articles. "We were told that we were irresponsible, that we were going to kill people, that we were in denial about what alcoholism really was," he told me. Marlatt, who died in 2011, said the findings called into question the foundations of the lucrative alcohol treatment industry. "It was all quite clear: There were interests people wanted to protect," he said.

The conflict over whether anyone identified by A.A. as an alcoholic (a self-selecting, broadly defined group) could ever drink in moderation has divided treatment experts ever since.

For proponents of twelve-step programs, the issue is doctrinal and beyond discussion. Decades before the Rand studies, the Big Book put it this way: "Physicians who are familiar with alcoholism agree there is no such thing as making a normal drinker out of an alcoholic. Science may one day accomplish this, but it hasn't done so yet."

Those who questioned this view—in the United States at least—were castigated. Marlatt, who was Canadian, was especially reviled. "Anyone who was considering the science of controlled drinking was accused of being in denial, of giving people permission to 'relapse,'" he told me. No one was *recommending* that alcoholics take up controlled drinking. The scientific findings merely reported that for some people, it was possible without advancing alcohol dependence.

•   •   •

At about the same time, another academic was beginning to question some of A.A.'s tenets, too. This time, however, the researcher challenged the group's suitability for herself. Sociologist Jean Kirkpatrick had joined the group as a graduate student at the University of Pennsylvania in the mid-1950s, and had stayed sober for three years. She worked through the steps, but little of the program's dogma made sense to her.

Kirkpatrick was an exemplary scholar who quickly earned the respect of her professors, as well as numerous honors and scholarships. But she was unable to internalize her accomplishments, convinced they were the result of a series of flukes. In 1958, when she became the first woman to receive one of Penn's most prestigious fellowships, her obsessive self-doubts took hold: Surely the university had made a terrible mistake.

She started drinking again, and didn't stop for another thirteen years.

Kirkpatrick came to realize that two of A.A.'s key messages—she was powerless over her drinking and must relinquish her ego in order to stop it—actually fueled her deep insecurities. As she thought about her drinking, she began to understand that her problem was an excess of humility—not a lack of it. The fundamental problem for her and other female drinkers was their lack of confidence, which society and culture reinforced. "For too long," she wrote in 1986, "programs for alcoholics have been designed by men, administered by men, dominated by men, and applied to women."

But what really rankled her was the notion of defenselessness against alcohol. Kirkpatrick felt that female problem drinkers needed a wholly different approach, and in the mid-1970s, she began a group called Women for Sobriety. She based its thirteen-step program on the writings of Ralph Waldo Emerson, her understanding of A.A., her experiences as a woman, and her knowledge of sociology. The program and its language are very much a product of the era, emphasizing self-assurance and independence, as well as reducing negative feelings a woman might have about her drinking and her perceived failures as a wife, mother, daughter, or professional. Like A.A., it promotes abstinence from alcohol. But Kirkpatrick's program encourages women to find spirituality within themselves—not from a higher power. It discourages the retelling of traumatic drinking stories, which Kirkpatrick believed only reinforced feelings of shame and worthlessness.

But her ideas were largely overlooked. Most treatment centers continued to use the same approach with men and women, relying on the twelve steps to treat a growing female clientele. By the early 1980s, the disgrace of being a woman with a drinking problem had begun to fade. Betty Ford left the White House, announced her recovery from pill and booze addictions, and founded a California facility that hewed to the twelve steps. Soon after it opened in 1982, the Betty Ford Center, which offered separate treatment quarters for men and women, was overwhelmed with requests from female patients, including some world-famous celebrities. Elizabeth Taylor and Liza Minnelli told their fans they "needed help" before they were admitted. Drew Barrymore checked in as a teenager. Elsewhere, Ann Richards campaigned for governor of Texas and openly discussed her drinking past. During her term, she established rehabilitation programs in prisons. On one prison visit, the governor introduced herself to the inmates by saying, "My name's Ann, and I'm an alcoholic."

The success stories of famous women were splashed across the pages of glossy magazines. It all seemed so simple: You admitted you had a problem, you went to rehab, you followed the twelve steps, and you got better. Between 1968 and 1989, the number of women in A.A. rose almost 60 percent, from 22 to 35 percent of all members. If the program helped Elizabeth Taylor, with her tangled love life and fragile health, it could surely work for women battling life's ordinary stresses.

Yet some feminists joined Kirkpatrick in their skepticism about the twelve-step gospel. In 1990, *Ms.* magazine published a piece by psychologist Charlotte Kasl called "The Twelve Step Controversy," in which she challenged its message to women, and later developed a sixteen-step recovery plan of her own. But to a great extent, Kirkpatrick's dissent remains an exception. Decades later, A.A. endures as the gold standard for recovery in America.

•   •   •

The nature of A.A. makes it difficult to analyze. While it conducts membership surveys every three years, A.A. keeps no records of who attends meetings. Members come and go, and are, of course, anonymous. Perhaps most important, A.A. itself is not a treatment; it is a support group. Researchers can observe A.A., but studying it scientifically poses huge challenges. Scientists like to conduct double-blind studies in which two statistically comparable groups are assembled. One receives the treatment, the other a placebo. Such an approach cannot be used for studying A.A., since participants are fully aware they are attending. Then there's the problem of measuring success. For A.A., it is abstinence, and a new way of thinking. But other approaches—such as harm reduction, which seeks to reduce or minimize the negative health and social consequences of alcohol or drug use—have different yardsticks, whether it is the ability to return to controlled drinking, or even drinking in such a way that poses no risks to others.

In the early days of A.A., Bill Wilson said he had observed a success rate of 75 percent among those who had come to A.A. and "really tried." About half of those who began attending meetings quit drinking in the first few weeks, and an additional 25 percent ultimately joined them in sobriety.

In the decades since, the sole source of data on A.A. membership has been A.A. Results are released to researchers sporadically, and one analysis of them appeared in the journal *Alcoholism Treatment Quarterly* in 2000. Researcher Don

McIntire, who had been given the data by A.A., found that only 5 percent of people who began attending A.A. meetings in 1990 were still participating a year later. This represented a significant decline from earlier surveys, which found that 25 percent of those who joined A.A. permanently stopped drinking.

Critics of A.A. immediately cited the 5 percent figure as proof of failings in the twelve-step approach. Actor Charlie Sheen even mentioned it while ranting on a radio talk show in 2011. But no less an authority than Dr. Drew Pinsky, a twelve-step proponent, admitted that Sheen "had a point" about A.A.'s success rates.

It was clear from the opening sentences of McIntire's paper that he anticipated criticism from A.A. members who view the group as the best way to address alcoholism. "The problem with the conclusions drawn from this data," McIntire wrote with homespun bluntness, "is that it does not sit well with the experience of seasoned A.A. members."

His author's note was also unusual: It listed neither his educational credentials nor a research institution, only his home address in Burbank, California.

A search turned up the telephone number instantly, and an older woman answered on the first ring. She identified herself as Carol McIntire, Don McIntire's widow. Her late husband, she said, had died in 2007 at the age of eighty-seven, an A.A. member for more than half his life. In his forties, he had sought treatment for alcoholism at Hazelden, where he forged friendships with many men who would go on to become prominent in A.A., Mrs. McIntire said.

She knew of the paper but said he hadn't talked about it much. "He kept his work to himself," she said. "That's how he was." She was aware of the controversy surrounding it, however, but said her mathematically oriented husband was clear on one thing: data. "It was black and white with him. Numbers were numbers," she said.

In this case, though, they revealed some unwelcome news. In fact, McIntire suggested structuring future studies to consider only those who completed A.A.'s ninety-day trial period, disregarding entirely the 81 percent of beginners who left before that point. (This is a little like clocking a triathlon that omits the swimming portion for athletes who hate getting wet. Of course the outcomes will be better.) If you followed McIntire's methodology, you would reach this conclusion: A.A. doesn't work for the vast majority of people who try it, but the small percentage who don't give up find it highly effective. A.A.'s most recent member survey, published in 2011, noted that 36 percent of the people attending meetings had been abstinent for more than a decade, powerful evidence that those who can stick to the program benefit from it.

Successful graduates of twelve-step programs vociferously defend their virtues, reacting to critics as if their religious beliefs had been questioned. On blogs and radio talk shows over the past decade, the debate has become confrontational, even ugly. Twitter followers snapped at Charlie Sheen; three A.A. members published their own rebuttal to McIntire's numbers. In it, they wrote: "The erroneous 10%, 5%, or less success rate myth for contemporary A.A. has proliferated without as much as a token challenge to its veracity or investigation of its origin. The topic of A.A. success or failure outcomes suffers from a great deal of anecdotal misinformation, misinterpretation, and editorializing." Somehow, the writers seem to have overlooked that the numbers came from A.A. itself.

Admirers and adherents of A.A. are quick to point out that it has saved the lives of "untold millions." To be sure, it offers a structure and a group of people who understand a drinker's frustrations and struggle. It provides a place to go, and a community that shares one's wishes for an undrunk future. It helps a person break away from drinking buddies and watering holes.

But many female problem drinkers, particularly stay-at-home mothers, drink in isolation. Meetings might help with many things, but it's hard to keep avoiding one's own kitchen. Since meetings are supposed to focus on alcohol alone, there is little tolerance of talk that veers toward sexual abuse, depression, or anxiety—proven predictors of risk for alcohol abuse among women.

To understand A.A. better, I attended about ten meetings in various parts of the country. I never spoke, and always went to open meetings that under A.A. protocol anyone can attend. Where I could, I found women's meetings in New Jersey, Manhattan, California, and Oregon. I started at the group's hub, the General Service Office on Manhattan's Upper West Side.

On Fridays, A.A.'s offices are thronged with visitors who have come for an 11 a.m. meeting in a large conference room. Afterward, they take a tour of the office, housed in a dull midcentury tower called the Interchurch Building, and visit the group's archives. Many pose for photos next to portraits of their heroes, or sitting in the couch said to be used by Wilson in the original New York office.

The first time I went, the place felt like Lourdes without the trail of canes. A group from Ireland stood reverentially before some framed documents. A woman blew into a Kleenex as she stood in front of Bill W.'s stony likeness, instructing her son to snap a photo. "Bill W. is like . . . our godfather!" she announced. A Miami woman from the meeting wept openly as she took a seat on Wilson's couch. "Tears of *felicidad*," she called out sunnily.

On the second visit, I was with a woman I know named Joy, a paralegal and community organizer who has been a member of A.A. for almost twenty-five years. Was it typical for people to be so moved? I asked her. She smiled. "Always," she said. "A.A. saved our lives." Joy is a striking woman in her early fifties who looks at least a decade younger, with unlined bronze skin and long black hair to her waist. She is unflinching in her assessment: "Critics call the program brainwashing, and in a way, it is. But you know what? Before I got here, my brain needed to be washed." Her parents both died of alcoholism, she said, but it wasn't enough to stop her from drinking. At the worst of it, Joy told me, she would reach to her nightstand and take a swig of tequila before she even got out of bed. "That was my life," she said. "To go from that to a college graduate with responsible jobs was unthinkable."

Unlike many A.A. members, she was unguarded about its statistics. "I'd say a 5 percent success rate is probably generous," Joy said, shrugging as she contemplated the menu in the boisterous Cuban restaurant where we went for lunch. "It taught me a different way to live. I had to stop lying, admit who and what I was," she said. She speaks softly, choosing her words carefully. "Because of A.A., I don't get up every day and destroy myself in a multitude of ways. But it's not for everybody."

With many other A.A. members, I quickly learned that posing certain questions is like criticizing your in-laws' politics in the middle of Thanksgiving dinner: You just don't do it.

But this was one point no one in A.A. seemed able to explain: Why, if alcoholism is a medical problem, do alcoholics need to rely most heavily on other alcoholics? It's one thing to get support; it's another to imbue that person, namely, a sponsor, with expert status in the process of getting better.

Do cardiologists need to have blocked arteries in order to successfully treat them? I have chronic sinus disease, but I don't need friends or even physicians who suffer from it—I only need a doctor trained in the most recent science, and who enlists me as a knowledgeable partner in the management of my condition. A.A. speaks of alcoholism being a spiritual, mental, and physical disease. But for many members, turning to physicians for help with an alcohol problem is taboo.

Within A.A., many women like the idea of a sponsor who has "been there"—someone who won't judge as she hears confessions of infidelity or deceit. In part because of this, Trysh Travis, a women's studies professor at the University of Florida who examines A.A. and its offshoots, describes A.A. as an "idealized mutual aid society." Travis is the author of *Language of the Heart: A Cultural History of the Recovery Movement from Alcoholics Anonymous to Oprah Winfrey*, and is a managing editor of *Points*, a blog for the Alcohol and Drugs History Society.

"Many people revere the idea of experience as the best teacher," Travis says. "But different people bring different skills to the table. You can be a masterful teacher without credentials." While privileged society may shun this notion, Travis says, many of those who have been victimized by elite institutions take comfort in it.

Yet because so many of its members see the organization as a savior—one that, as Travis puts it, made the difference between freedom and prison, home and the street, life and death—it inspires some powerful feelings. "There is a hagiographic tendency within A.A.," she says. "And what's unfortunate is that for many of these people, their personal experience becomes a closed-mindedness." Such stridency is not unique to A.A., of course: It happens when people alter their behaviors to conform to new belief systems, whether it's feminism or veganism. "They say, 'I got a message, I was able to change my thinking in the most powerful, meaningful way, and I want to spread the good news—and if you don't like it there is something wrong with you.'"

But is it possible that some problem drinking is just that—problem drinking—and not a progressive disease? At the end of her life, Elizabeth Taylor was a once-a-week regular at a West Hollywood bar called the Abbey, where she downed tequila shots and watermelon martinis. Did that make her unrecovered? What if you struggle with drinking but don't believe you are powerless?

Mark Willenbring, a Minnesota psychiatrist who for five years served as director of treatment research at NIAAA, has spent much of his adult life trying to bring rigor to the question of how to treat problem drinkers. He chooses his words carefully, which is why I was surprised when he told me it is pointless to try to quantify the efficacy of A.A.

"You can't really study whether it works, because people who affiliate find it useful, and will therefore report that it does work [for them]. People who don't affiliate will report that it doesn't work," he says. "It's like trying to study the 'effectiveness' of yoga, prayer, or confiding in a friend. It's really the wrong question to ask."

Early colonists drank beer, hard cider, and rum daily. Alcohol was safer than water, which was often contaminated with raw sewage. Here, some Dutch settlers in New Amsterdam celebrate the New Year.

The Mother of our Country liked to party. Martha Washington's collection of five hundred recipes included fifty for alcoholic drinks, and even a few hangover cures. One concoction called for plunging the meat of a raw, castrated rooster into two gallons of ale. Historians estimate adults in the eighteenth century drank about a gallon of beer a day.

3

By the late nineteenth century, much of the nation had clean drinking water, and religious reformers turned their sights on banning booze. Women were its earliest and most ardent supporters. Here, a temperance worker records the names of those entering a saloon.

Carry Nation believed she had divine orders to smash up bars with an axe, which she called "hatchetations." Nation described herself as "a bulldog running along at the feet of Jesus, barking at what He doesn't like." Between 1900 and 1910, she was arrested thirty times for vandalizing saloons.

4

5

Many young women in the Prohibition era enjoyed a radical new independence. They went to college, joined the workforce in large numbers, and dressed, danced, and drank in scandalously modern ways. They also had clever ways of hiding liquor.

Lucille Ball agre

ROMA WINE AND SODA

ROM
Estate

Postwar imagery of women and alcohol was often at odds. California wine makers were eager to promote their product to American consumers as an everyday drink. In the late 1940s, they brought out Lucy as a pitchwoman.

In this friendly, freedom-loving land of ours... *Beer Belongs—Enjoy It!*

BEER AND ALE—AMERICA'S BEVERAGES OF MODERATION
Sponsored by the United States Brewers Foundation ... Chartered 1862

Likewise, beer producers portrayed beer as a wholesome grown-up drink that was also patriotic. Hundreds of Rockwellian images like these ran in magazines between 1945 and 1956.

At the same time, it was clear that women who drank too much would lose everything that mattered in the strict mores of postwar society. In the biopic *I'll Cry Tomorrow*, Susan Hayward portrays the drunken torment of the actress and singer Lillian Roth.

In *The Days of Wine and Roses*, Lee Remick's drinking prompts her family to cut off her access to her child.

Alcoholics Anonymous grew rapidly in the 1940s as the remedy for alcoholism. Marty Mann, left, was one of its first women. She used her skills as a public relations executive to help publicize its story. Here, she is with E. M. Jellinek, an alcohol researcher whose CV included fake degrees. Working closely with Jellinek, Mann helped craft the message of alcoholism as a disease that had a precise trajectory and treatment.

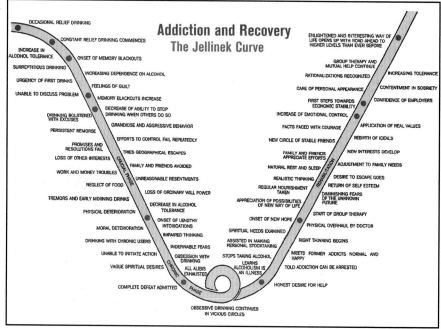

Proponents of Alcoholics Anonymous cited scientific-looking studies to bolster the narrative that A.A. was the most effective treatment of alcoholic dependency. Charts named for Jellinek's work appeared in magazines and in doctor's offices, but they were based on a self-selected group of A.A. members, none of whom were women.

In the 1960s and '70s, California's laid-back culture influenced the country in music, food, surfing—and wine. Napa Valley wine growers promoted their product as part of a healthy life, and they targeted a new generation of customers: women.

14

In *Cougar Town*, Courteney Cox's character Jules loves her gigantic wine vessels so much, she has a memorial service for the shards of one that breaks.

15

Annette Bening as the on-edge doctor, Nic, in *The Kids Are All Right*. Her drinking is a source of tension in her relationship with her partner, who is constantly monitoring her consumption.

Still, researchers do—perhaps because it is so ubiquitous. A comprehensive analysis in the *Cochrane Review,* a prestigious British journal, compared A.A. and twelve-step programs to other treatments, and found that A.A. and related programs were no more effective at reducing alcohol abuse than any other method.

In the early 1990s, an NIAAA study called Project MATCH compared twelve-step treatment with cognitive behavioral therapy, which teaches patients skills that might help avoid drinking triggers, and motivational enhancement therapy, which helps patients generate their own incentives to quit. The $30 million study found all treatments equally effective for both genders—and generated immediate criticism. Psychologist and author Stanton Peele noted that the study hadn't included a control group of untreated problem drinkers who also wanted to stop drinking. Alan Marlatt called it "poorly conceived," and said it allowed addiction specialists to project their own views onto treatment.

Many researchers remain dismayed at the expense and design of the study. In a reanalysis of the data published in 2005, researchers Robert Cutler and David Fishbain wrote that most of the patient improvements noted in the study were interpreted as the result of effective treatment—when in fact they were due mainly to the motivations of the patients themselves. And, as Willenbring pointed out, the studies were largely conducted in academic settings, where the counselors were well trained, highly monitored, and had extensive clinical supervision. In fact, he said, most treatment facilities rely heavily on lower-paid alcohol counselors, many of whom have only a high school education.

The study overlooked another important complication, especially for women with histories of sexual abuse. As more and more women entered twelve-step programs in rehab and A.A., they faced yet another difficulty as they entered coed facilities and attended mixed-gender meetings. The "sex thing," as Bill Wilson's friend Tom Powers had dubbed it, began to emerge as a national problem.

There has been little if any open discussion of sexual predation by participants in the nation's brand-name recovery movement. The group's adoption of the term "thirteenth-stepping"—the euphemism for a broad range of behavior ranging from creepy come-ons to statutory rape—implies it is a behavior to be expected. Its prevalence is an open secret.

6 *The Thirteenth Step*

For years, Monica Richardson, a singer and actress in Los Angeles, spoke to no one about her early experiences in A.A. She felt she had been naive, even partly responsible for what happened. Best to move ahead. It had been a rocky period in her life. Richardson pushed the memories into the deepest recesses of her mind, to the point that they almost didn't exist. After a few years in A.A., she came to believe that she was fundamentally broken. She never bought into the group's clichés, but this passage from the Big Book made sense: "We are like men who have lost their legs; they never grow new ones."

Richardson had a wild adolescence in 1970s New York, pounding shots in bars, smoking pot, and experimenting with sex. In high school, she was hospitalized after a serious drinking binge. A social worker assigned to the case warned her:

"You'd better watch this, or you're headed for serious trouble." Using money she'd saved from a babysitting job, Richardson decided to leave the chaos of New York for Hawaii, where her father lived at the time. The calm of her new surroundings eluded her: Isolated, anxious, and lonely, she drank to excess almost every night. One evening at a party, she drank so much she stripped off her clothes and dove into the pitch-black ocean. She woke up the next morning doubled over in stomach pain, and scared as she tried to recall the night's events. The social worker's words haunted her. "Am I an alcoholic?" Richardson wondered.

Two weeks later, a man approached her as she sunbathed on a beach, and began telling her about the kinship and peace he had found through A.A. "It seemed like a message from the universe," she says. She joined him and his friends at a meeting. The tales people told of hitting rock bottom terrified her. Soon, she was convinced that she, too, was an alcoholic—and that without A.A., she would meet a hopeless end. She was eighteen years old.

It is salient to point out that today Richardson, in her midfifties, is a statuesque stunner, with huge green eyes, curly auburn hair, and a husky contralto. Perhaps this is why a half dozen men rushed forward after her first meeting and offered to guide her through recovery. One of those who approached her was a handsome, bearded man I'll call Ken. Seven years her senior, Ken wasted no time inviting her on a hike. The two hit it off, and soon Richardson was spending most days—and every night—with Ken, who worked as an addictions counselor at a methadone clinic.

Thrilled with sobriety and her new community, she devoured the Big Book, attended daily meetings, and did the first few steps on her own. Ken was like no one she had ever met in New York: He sang folk songs as he strummed his guitar, quoted from *Siddhartha,* and massaged deep knots out of her neck with his suntanned hands. Richardson felt as if she had found a new spiritual home, and partner.

A.A. discourages sexual relationships between longtime members and newcomers. That advice is mentioned in the Twelve Traditions, the principles A.A. describes as the fellowship's common spiritual guidelines. The theory is that a person struggling to quit drinking and put his or her life back together can't make sound decisions, and that there is an inevitable imbalance between A.A. beginners and those who have been sober for years. Richardson was unaware of the rule, and Ken certainly didn't tell her. Ken had been in the program five years; Richardson, less than a month. She had not yet asked anyone to be her sponsor.

A few weeks into their relationship, the couple flew from Oahu to Maui for a weekend. Late one night at a rustic motel, geckos darting through the jalousies, Ken asked Richardson how she had come to be so sexually confident at such a young age. At the time, Richardson was working through A.A.'s fourth step, taking a "searching and fearless moral inventory" of her character defects: fears, resentments, sexual conduct, and ways in which she had harmed others. Ken urged her to share her history. "Let it all out," he said.

Richardson's accounting of herself included sexual encounters she had come to regret, including some evenings with a group of swingers. As Richardson poured out dark moments from her past, Ken withdrew his hand from Richardson's knee, his face twisted with horror. "That's disgusting," he told her, rising abruptly from the bed. "This is over."

The reproach took Richardson aback, particularly because it came from someone who preached free love and boasted about his dozens of partners. He had encouraged Richardson to continue on A.A.'s path, which counsels members to confess their most shameful secrets as a way to liberate them from the malady of excess drinking. "You are only as sick as your secrets," an A.A. slogan says. The point of working through your most toxic transgressions with another alcoholic, after all, is because the fellow drunk has "been there." The newcomer is less likely to feel judged in the company of other reforming drunks.

"You don't walk into A.A. because your life is going great," she says now. "You walk into A.A. because you are desperate. You think it will be a safe place, with people who are healthier than you. And A.A. tells you you're powerless, your thinking is flawed, you have defects, to shut up and listen," she says. "You're fuzzy-headed, you're confused, you're clearing booze from your brain. You don't know how to have relationships without alcohol, so you do what they say. They've been there. They're there to help, right? Alcoholics helping alcoholics."

But as Marty Mann had pointed out, female alcoholics face a double standard. Richardson booked a flight back to Oahu, retrieved her bike at Ken's, and sobbed as she pedaled back to her father's. She went home to New York, where she attended A.A. several times a week. She returned to Hawaii ten months later, and resumed meeting with her first A.A. group.

A few weeks from her nineteenth birthday, two men at the meeting persuaded her to have sex with them. She trusted the men, and consented. They were more than two decades older, and had been sober for many years—one would go on to be-

come a counselor at a respected Hawaiian treatment center. As she tried to live her life without alcohol, she thought that the men might have insights on the inner peace she believed she lacked. Instead, she felt used and humiliated.

Determined to put the incidents behind her forever, Richardson switched groups, and stayed in Hawaii for another seven years before leaving for Los Angeles to launch her career as a singer and actress. Despite her negative experiences in A.A., she remained wedded to the group's ideas, and the notion that she was an alcoholic.

Once in L.A., she found a women's group she liked, which helped to root her in her new city. Over the next fifteen years, she established herself as a singer, recording folk music in two albums, and studied at Groundlings and Playhouse West, two prestigious acting schools. Through her work, she met and married a television engineer, and had two sons. As a tired thirty-something working mother, Richardson found that her interest in sex plummeted, and the marriage began to falter. She and her husband sought counseling, and the therapist gently asked about her sexual past. The questions set alight some disturbing memories from her early time in A.A. and along with that, the molestations she had suffered for years at the hands of her great-aunt. In sessions with a separate therapist, Richardson learned how to channel her anger productively, and to shed guilt for experiences, like sexual abuse, over which she had had no control.

Like many victims of childhood sexual abuse, Richardson had spent much of her life feeling voiceless around people she perceived as powerful. In therapy, she began to realize why it had been so difficult for her to say no to the sexual advances of the older men she met in A.A. The relationship, she began to see, was a familiar one. As a child, her molester, a great-aunt who lived a block away, had helped to raise Richardson and her two siblings as part of an extended family. After school, the great-aunt often babysat for the three kids, getting them ready for dinner and bathing them. She frequently took them to her own small apartment to spend the night, where Richardson shared her bed. It was understood that Richardson was never to discuss her aunt's inappropriate nighttime touching.

The episodes also set in place a dynamic that would take Richardson years to recognize as harmful. In public, her late great-aunt was a loving, protective authority figure, revered and respected in Inwood, their close-knit Manhattan neighborhood. In private, she violated intimate boundaries.

Studies show that Richardson's experiences are common. Sexual abuse, as either a child or an adult, is one of the largest risk factors for women who become problem drinkers. Some researchers have found that women who were victimized as children are three times more likely to develop alcohol or other chemical dependence problems than women who were not.

As adults, it is also common for such women to be preyed upon in twelve-step programs by those who are purporting to help them heal. Psychologist Charlotte Davis Kasl writes that the A.A. old-timer who sexually exploits a new member is replicating the twisted bond between a child and a sexually abusive relative. Lacking the power to speak up, particularly when the trusted figure tells the child she is "special," the child accepts the behavior as normal. So when an older A.A. member encourages a sexual relationship, many newcomers, already accustomed to this pattern, find it difficult to say no.

Since the group's first days in Akron, A.A. has advised

new heterosexual members to seek sponsors from among their own gender while encouraging gays to do the opposite. These are only suggestions, and A.A. makes clear that it has no authority in enforcing them

Another recommendation, also stemming from the early days, is that women should attend women-only groups. This is often not practical. While one-third of A.A.'s membership is female, the number of women-only meetings is scant: A 2010 sociology journal found that only 3 percent of the twenty thousand weekly meetings in a large metropolitan area were for women only.

Whatever precautions are being taken, they don't appear to be working. A 2003 study in the *Journal of Addictions Nursing* found that half of the women surveyed said they had experienced various forms of thirteenth stepping, from groping to pressure for dates or sexual liaisons. Four percent said they had been raped by a sponsor or fellow A.A. member.

The advances typically take place like this: At coffee after the meeting, a man is chatty and friendly, asking a newcomer if she has any questions, or needs any help with the steps. "You're not in a bar, where you're prepared for guys on the prowl," Richardson says. "You're at an A.A. meeting with people who are supposed to show you how to live in a healthier way." (I witnessed some of this behavior myself. At the meetings I attended, I always dressed dowdily—and I'm in my late forties. After a meeting in suburban New Jersey, one man followed me up the stone steps of a church, asking if I was new. I told him I was a journalist—"Just here to listen!"—but it didn't stop him from thrusting his card into my hand and inviting me to come see his new Mercedes. He offered to take me for a "ride.")

I also read the creepy diary of Sean Calahan, a Montana sex offender who used A.A. as his personal pickup joint. In April 2012, police found that Calahan, on probation for the sexual assault of a twelve-year-old girl, was violating the conditions of his parole by initiating sexual relationships with multiple members of the women in his A.A. group. In a journal entry called "Sean's Dark Side," he wrote how he preyed on A.A. members: "Will take sex where I can get it. Whoever I can trick or use. Usually women early in sobriety 'cause they are the most vunerable. They have the most insecuritys so just a few words and a little care and they fall rite in to my trap. Its not there falt but I make them think it is there falt and tell them I love them and everything will be okay."

This, too, fits a pattern, and manipulators like Calahan are likely to know it, since, as Kasl points out, women who have been sexually taken advantage of are nonetheless often afraid to leave the group. She says this replicates an earlier relationship in which abusers often warned their victims to keep silent. So they did, afraid that they might be punished. When these women are sexually exploited in A.A., they repeat the pattern, Kasl found. "Fearing relapse, rejection, or being shamed," she wrote, they "continue with the group or deny their internal wisdom. As a result they deepen the wounds inflicted by their family of origin."

Richardson believed that without A.A., she would be "struck drunk," a permanent condition from which she might never recover. In fact, she immersed herself in the group, serving as a sponsor for several women, a public information chairwoman, a group secretary and treasurer, and founder of a group for young people. For many years, she went into prisons to oversee groups for convicted felons and juvenile delinquents.

In 2009, she was elected a general service representative, or GSR, an unpaid but important position within A.A. that transmits ideas and opinions between a local group and others in A.A. Richardson's home group of mostly women seemed cozy and safe. What had happened to her in Hawaii, she believed, was isolated bad luck. It had been a confusing time— for the country, for her, and for a group trying to help some of society's most desperate people.

•   •   •

More than thirty years later, Richardson learned differently when a twenty-two-year-old woman named Gwen began attending her home meeting. The evening Gwen first spoke, her words came between sobs. When she first joined A.A., Gwen said, she had no car, no license, "really not even a life," so she walked to and from meetings. As she tiptoed into a life without alcohol, Gwen told herself to be especially on guard about the opposite sex. When men in the group asked her if she wanted a ride home, she would always just flash the small can of mace she kept in her purse and smile. "I'm fine," she would tell them. "I can go by myself."

An especially unrelenting member would not take no for an answer, pestering Gwen one night to get into his car. "No, I already told you, I'm fine walking," she said. As Gwen marched homeward, he circled the block several times, asking her to get into the car every time he passed. "I don't want you to walk," he called out. Finally, worn down, and believing he had her best interests in mind, Gwen said yes and climbed in. When they got to Gwen's driveway, the man came to the door.

The man had five years' sobriety to Gwen's few weeks, and he convinced her that she should let him spend the night. He did, and stayed for months, rent-free, insisting that it—and sex on demand—was part of Gwen's "service" to other alcoholics. With him, the man promised, Gwen would certainly stay sober. Instinctively, she knew the situation was wrong, but old-timers at her meeting told her daily that her misguided "best thinking" had landed her in A.A. When Gwen dared question the appropriateness of the relationship with her female sponsor, her sponsor asked, "Well, what's your part in it?" The term is A.A. shorthand for a fundamental tenet—that alcoholics have a "part" in all misfortunes that befall them.

As soon as the meeting was over, Richardson hurried across the room to comfort Gwen. "I'm so sorry that you've had to go through this," Richardson told her. "I was abused by some members in my early days, too. I didn't know that kind of thing still happened." Gwen looked at her, stunned. "It's not only me," she said. "This is going on everywhere!" For the next several weeks, Gwen and Richardson went to mixed meetings throughout Los Angeles. Richardson was shocked to hear incident after incident of wrongdoing: rapes, unwanted touching, harassment. She documented many young women's claims in videotaped interviews.

At home one night on her computer, Richardson typed in "thirteenth step in A.A." She found several blogs that were critical of A.A., and links to 2007 articles in *Newsweek* and the *Washington Post* that detailed the sexual and emotional abuse of young women at a cultlike A.A. group in Washington, D.C., called Midtown. Richardson was shocked by what she read. In the stories, the young women recounted how they were pressured to have sex with many A.A. members, but especially with the group leader, Michael Quinones. A woman identified as Kristen told the *Post* that her psychologist had referred her to the group at age seventeen. Soon, her sponsor instructed her to have sex with Quinones as a way to solidify her sobriety, and once Kristen became a sponsor she encouraged the women she was helping to do the same. "I pimped [them] out," she told the *Post*.

Women who belonged to the group said they were ordered off their psychiatric medication, told to stop seeing their therapists, and allowed to visit family members only in the company of other Midtown members. The allegations suggested not only a frightening level of control, but also a codified thirteenth step.

Police concluded no crime had been committed, since the young women in question were over the age of sixteen and therefore consenting adults. The young women told police that sexual relations between teenagers and older men was rampant, but were unwilling to admit they were victims themselves.

Richardson recognized that much of what had gone on at Midtown violated A.A.'s traditions, including the suggestion for same-sex sponsors and the idea that newcomers should choose sponsors, not be assigned to them.

Midtown's opposition to members taking psychiatric meds like antidepressants is not unusual. While A.A. instructs members not to "play doctor," many members take it upon themselves to counsel against ingesting any psychoactive drugs, even those prescribed by a physician.

This view is at odds with modern psychiatry. If patients stop taking antidepressants abruptly, they can experience unpleasant side effects. But they don't create dependency in the traditional sense, since they don't induce euphoria or cause people to act inappropriately in order to obtain them.

I asked A.A.'s General Service Office how the group enforces the guidelines laid out in the Twelve Traditions and other documents. Does it, for example, ever expel a local organization like Midtown, which violated a host of A.A. standards? She replied in an e-mail: "The Traditions are not rules—they are spiritual principles that guide A.A. members in their relations with each other and with the community," wrote Mary C., public information officer at the General Service Office, A.A.'s headquarters in Manhattan. "There is no central mechanism in A.A. to 'enforce' the Traditions or any existing guidelines or, for that matter, most anything at all."

When ex-Midtown members contacted the New York office with complaints about the group's tactics, the GSO said it had no authority over local groups. A.A. is not a franchiser like McDonald's or Burger King. Each group is free to structure itself as it wishes. Reports flow from individual groups to districts, from districts to areas, and from areas to the GSO in Manhattan. Every local group elects a general service representative to represent the group at district meetings, and each area in the U.S. and Canada elects a delegate to attend an annual conference, which holds votes on "matters of importance." All of these positions are held by unpaid volunteers.

As Richardson scrolled through the *Newsweek* and *Washington Post* stories, she felt her face flush and her stomach lurch. At that point in her life, A.A. was her anchor, a nurturing family whose virtues far outweighed its flaws. She was committed to the fellowship that had served as her beacon. The group had shaped much of her adult life. Her first sponsor, a kind, loving woman, had encouraged her to develop her talents as a performer. When she had singing gigs at nightclubs, buddies from her group showed up by the dozens.

In late 2009, Richardson reached out to a friend who had worked as a paid staff member at the GSO for a decade. He listened intently as Richardson recounted the experiences she had documented, and suggested that she meet a trustee, whom I will call Mr. X. The friend handed Richardson some documents. One was a 2001 memo from Australia's General Service Board that outlined how to halt spiritual, sexual, and financial predation within the group—including barring predators from meetings, if needed, and notifying the police. It said that older members and office holders had a "moral obligation" to help protect vulnerable members, and possibly even a legal one.

In 2002, Richardson learned, Britain's thirty-four hundred A.A. groups had adopted a "code of conduct" regarding sexual behavior, after British newspapers had reported that a number of groups were under police investigation for allegations involving predators who operated telephone help lines. They would visit the homes of callers under the guise of offering help, and then sexually assault them.

The phone lines were supposed to be staffed by members with appropriate experience and long-term sobriety. But a British A.A. memo, leaked to the press, revealed that those rules were often broken by "a small minority of men and women who operate with sick but hidden agendas." It warned that "the organization has the potential to become a breeding ground for predatory behavior."

In the leaked documents, A.A. nonalcoholic trustee Geoffrey Brown, an Anglican priest, likened the abuse within A.A. to the sexual abuse scandals roiling the Catholic Church.

"The problem with caring communities is that, by definition, they are bound to attract the kind of vulnerable person that a very small minority can prey upon. . . . It is because of this fact that such groups need constantly to be on their guard against any conduct that takes advantage of the powerless.'"

The British behavioral guidelines include instructions for members and newcomers to have third parties present during talks and home visits. They warn specifically against bullying, harassment, and discrimination, and direct groups to hold frequent meetings to discuss member conduct. The guidelines conclude: "Failure to challenge and stop inappropriate behaviour gives the offender permission to repeat the offensive behaviour and encourages others to follow suit."

Fewer than 1 percent of Britain's A.A. groups objected to the new rules.

So Richardson felt hopeful when she pored over one of the other documents her friend had given her, a confidential seven-page memo Mr. X had sent in 2007 to A.A.'s Subcommittee on Vulnerable Members. Written against the backdrop of the *Washington Post* and *Newsweek* stories and reports of pedophile priests, it detailed multiple instances of sexual abuse within A.A., and called for the group to draft clear guidelines to protect members from predators. Under no circumstances, he wrote, should the group allow its longstanding traditions of anonymous participation to cover up criminal behavior by members. "There is confusion about taking legal action against perpetrators because the victims think they will be breaking anonymity, fear retribution . . . and won't be believed."

In his letter to the subcommittee, Mr. X acknowledged that while women may also be predators, "the vast majority of situations appear to involve men preying on underage girls." His language was blunt: "A man in A.A. who becomes sexually involved with a minor . . . is taking advantage of a child at a most vulnerable time in her life, and committing a serious crime."

He then listed several examples of sexual abuse for which he had direct evidence. They included:

- A thirty-five-year-old woman was raped at age fifteen by a member in his twenties. Her sponsor told her to "pray for him."

- A woman with long-term sobriety asked for guidance after learning that a man in A.A. had molested her daughter. Mr. X advised her to go to the police, but the woman feared breaking A.A.'s promise of anonymity to the abuser.

- Another woman said she had been tied up and raped by a man who broke into her house after meeting her in A.A. Her sponsor told her to "forgive him."

- A speaker at an A.A. convention was found having sex with the fifteen-year-old daughter of another A.A. member attending the convention.

To demonstrate the persistence of the problem, Mr. X quoted a 1993 letter published in the *Grapevine*. It was written by a woman whose fifteen-year-old daughter had been impregnated by an A.A. old-timer. "Those with maturity and leadership in A.A. have a responsibility to be very vocal about the dangers of Thirteenth Stepping. No more turning a blind eye to this problem," the woman wrote.

Richardson knew she had an ally, and immediately called Mr. X. Fueled by the scandal at the Midtown group in Washington, Mr. X's support, and her own documentation, Richardson was certain she could spur action. Members of her women's home group were outraged when they learned of the documents, and the systemic manner in which sexual abuse had flourished within A.A. "We were sick about this," she says. "I thought everyone would be."

She was mistaken.

In October 2009, more than two years after the trustee wrote his memo, A.A.'s six-member Subcommittee on Vulnerable Members responded with a one-page letter. Its sentences were lawyerly but the intent was clear. A.A. headquarters in New York would do nothing to set standards for American groups and would accept no liability for anything that went awry at A.A. meetings.

Here's the key passage: "The subcommittee members agree that the General Service Board in its position at the bottom of the A.A. service structure would not have a role in setting any behavioral policy or guideline for the A.A. groups or members in regards to protecting any vulnerable member including minors coming into A.A. The A.A. groups and A.A. service entities such as Areas and Districts are autonomous and direct and guide their own affairs. The General Service Board has no authority, legal or otherwise, to control or direct the behavior of A.A. members and groups."

Protecting members was up to local groups. "It is hoped that the areas, districts, and groups will discuss this important topic and seek ways through sponsorship, workshops and assemblies and committee meetings to raise awareness in the Fellowship and encourage the creation of as safe an environment as possible for the newcomer, minors and other members or potential members who may be vulnerable."

Richardson gathered additional evidence. In late 2009, she wrote a seven-page letter of her own, describing five additional rape cases she had learned of in recent months, and sent it to all members of A.A.'s board, as well as five paid staff members at Alcoholics Anonymous World Service. No one responded.

She approached her district chair about getting on the agenda to speak at a district meeting. "You can't just ask to do that," he told her. "You have to go to a committee meeting first and get their approval." A few weeks later, she and a friend from her home group attended the committee meeting, and asked to be put on the agenda. All voted no. "This could hurt A.A.'s name," they told her. "This is an outside issue."

That term has special meaning in the A.A. view of alcoholism, and it explains a lot about the organization's reluctance to address the issues of sexual misconduct. Its roots lie in the fate of the nineteenth-century organization, the Washingtonians. The group allowed politicians and temperance reformers who were not alcoholics to join the group, and soon it became embroiled in the country's other pressing political battle, abolition. Infighting about slavery ultimately led to the group's demise, and as Wilson began to sketch A.A.'s blueprint, he took note. In the Twelve Traditions, the group sets specific rules for refraining from all "outside issues" that are unrelated to the group's primary goal: helping others stop drinking. The group's Tenth Tradition states: "No A.A. group or member should ever, in such a way as to implicate A.A., express any opinion on outside controversial issues—particularly those of politics, alcohol reform, or sectarian religion. The Alcoholics Anonymous groups oppose no one. Concerning such matters they can express no views whatever."

This broad guideline is considered by many to include all matters apart from alcohol, including sexual relationships.

Hearing this, Richardson was incredulous. "Outside issue? We're talking about women getting groped at meetings, sexually harassed at meetings. This is not an outside issue!"

Twenty women in her group signed a letter so that as a GSR, Richardson might address the topic at an upcoming area meeting. She was granted one minute of speaking time at the day-long January 2010 meeting. "I realize that this sounds like a very small amount of time," the area chairman wrote in an e-mail.

After that meeting, two people came up to tell her they knew of rapes in their local groups.

A few weeks later, an editor of the *Grapevine* called her from New York, saying she had seen her letter. She offered to publish Richardson's tale from Hawaii—but not the newer stories of the five rapes—in the newsletter. Richardson demurred. "Why would I want to talk about something that happened in 1975 when the point was informing people that it was still happening today?" she recalls wondering.

Mr. X advised Richardson to organize a workshop on predatory behavior. She again approached her district chairman to ask if she could make an announcement about her workshop. "No," he told her. "You can't."

Richardson is a fearsome woman with a thick skin—years of acting training had taught her not to take rejection personally—and this time, she would not take no for an answer. Fed up with the many obstacles she had encountered, she spoke up anyway, asking members at the meeting if they wanted fliers to the upcoming workshop. Only twenty-five of the seventy-five people assembled held out their hands. The hostility, she recalls, was palpable.

Richardson redoubled her efforts. She investigated more cases and started a blog, *Stop13stepinaa.com*. She published a pamphlet titled "Make A.A. Safer" and handed it out at area meetings, and, buoyed by the support of Mr. X, began planning a workshop about predatory behavior. She met with women in Spanish-speaking groups, who told her horror stories of their own. They translated Richardson's materials into Spanish and distributed them widely. She approached the area and district chairs to have them post her workshop on the Los Angeles–area website calendar. They declined. So she trudged from meeting to meeting in an attempt to publicize her workshop.

She pressed on, eventually getting permission to speak for ten minutes at a larger area assembly. A handful of people voiced support, but many complained that open discussion of the matter would hurt A.A.'s reputation.

Late in the summer of 2010, Richardson heard that a Honolulu A.A. member and her daughter had been murdered by a violent Iraq veteran ordered into A.A. by a judge.

Richardson learned that the troubled veteran, Clayborne Conley, had briefly dated Kristine Cass after meeting her in A.A. Conley, once convicted of the assault and "terroristic threatening" of an ex-girlfriend, struggled with post-traumatic stress disorder. He spent ten months in a Hawaii state mental hospital, agreeing to attend A.A. as part of his conditional 2009 release. Friends in his A.A. group told a newspaper reporter that Conley was smart and funny, and had no inkling of his record. Cass, a Honolulu marketing consultant, was unaware, too, until she broke off the relationship. Then, he began calling her at all hours and showing up at her workplace, demanding to see her. On August 19, 2010, she told a friend that she planned to seek a temporary restraining order against him. Hours later, Conley ripped apart the security bars on Cass's windows, broke into her house, and shot her, her daughter, and a neighbor's dog before killing himself.

Richardson was stunned when some fellow A.A. members dismissed the murder-suicide as something that could "happen anywhere." She finds this logic skewed. A.A. presents itself as a healing community, a fellowship in which people voluntarily help each other. What, she asks, would stop A.A. from warning members that some of those in the meetings were attending not because they desired sobriety, but because a court had ordered them there? "Why wouldn't the organization want a members' safety statement read before every meeting, just to make the fellowship aware of potential dangers?"

Her outspokenness took a toll. By the time she was ending her stint as a GSR, Richardson's A.A. friends had stopped coming to her singing engagements and her poolside karaoke parties. The more outspoken she became, the more ostracized she felt. For more than three decades, A.A. had been Richardson's foundation, providing a social circle and professional contacts.

None of the evidence that motivated Richardson seemed to matter to many others: not the trustee's letter, not Richardson's new documentation, not her position as a GSR, not the fact that A.A. groups abroad had confronted the issue and acted a decade earlier.

"I went through every channel I could possibly go through," she says. "A.A. tells you that it's an upside-down organization, where the groups have the power, but that's just not true."

• • •

Richardson left A.A. as soon as her term was finished, in early 2011, and is making a documentary about the experiences of many women in the group. Little seems to have changed since then regarding A.A.'s response to the issue of violence against women. In late 2011, I spoke to a former A.A. board member who was familiar with the internal memo and insisted on not being identified. The former trustee likened the possibility of A.A. enacting swift reform to turning a battleship on a dime. Unlike Richardson, the former trustee seemed resigned to the group's inability to act with any sense of urgency. "It's a little harsh," the former board member told me hesitantly, "but women have been getting raped since A.A. started."

Not much appears to have changed in the culture of Washington's Midtown group. Marc Fisher, the *Washington Post* writer who covered the scandal, told me he still receives calls and e-mails from family members of those ensnared in the group, desperate for help to get them out. Quinones, who was dying of cancer when the stories appeared, never responded to Fisher's requests for an interview. But some of his friends did, and told Fisher privately that what he had reported was just the "tip of the iceberg."

Ellen Dye, a Washington-area psychologist, concurred. In 2006, Dye wrote an open letter to the D.C. recovery community about how members of Midtown had abused two of her clients. Like many mental health professionals, Dye has seen A.A. achieve some notable successes. But she says the events at Midtown have given her pause. "It's still going on," she says. Some of her clients have told her that nothing has changed.

Women are hesitant to discuss sexual abuse openly, and they're even more reluctant when they've been branded as alcoholics. "Who's going to believe a drunk girl when she says she's been raped?" asks Amy Lee Coy, a Los Angeles singer and author of a book about her own recovery from alcohol abuse, *From Death Do I Part*. Coy was barely out of detox at a tony twelve-step facility in Malibu before a counselor made a pass at her. Louise, a Cleveland lawyer who left A.A. in 2007 after members of her home group made excuses for the Midtown scandal, says double standards endure. She likens it to the Penn State sex abuse case. "It's one thing when cute, innocent little boys are being raped by a nasty-looking old man, but quite another when nasty barflies are getting raped by other nasty barflies."

A.A. loyalists often scoff at those who say they've been victims of the thirteenth step. In a forum on the anti-A.A. blog *Orange Papers,* a commenter wrote: "You are responsible for who you shack up with, give money to, or move in with. You can blame A.A. or anyone else all you wish, but the responsibility lies with each individual. Even if you've drank and drugged yourself to a state of vulnerability and naive desperation, who's [*sic*] fault is that?"

Gwen, the young woman Richardson met in 2009, addressed that point on Richardson's weekly Internet radio show, which attracts thousands of L.A. listeners.

"What was 'my part'?" Gwen asked when speaking of the man who demanded sex as part of her "service" to other alcoholics. "My part was that I was twenty-two. My part was that I showed up at A.A. My part," she concluded, "was believing people who told me my 'best thinking' was wrong."

• • •

Richardson and others argue that A.A. is in much the same position as the Catholic Church in the 1990s. The signs of sexual misconduct are unmistakable. Yet the leadership fears that taking action will be an admission of liability. And women remain reluctant to press charges.

Among the predominantly male leadership and rank and file of A.A., there is little appetite to deal with this issue. When I was on a tour of the General Service Office in 2010, I identified myself as a journalist at work on a book about women and alcohol. My companion, a longtime A.A. member, introduced me to some staff members, including one who had just returned from a meeting with A.A. leaders in eastern Europe. "Thirteenth stepping is a big problem over there," he said, out of the blue. My companion told me later she was "shocked" that he had volunteered the information.

When I mentioned the problem to others, I heard these defenses: "All recovery communities involve sexual abuse." "The sexual appetites of alcoholics 'go haywire' when they're newly sober and they have to get that rush from somewhere, so they seek sex." "There's no way to keep deviants out of any group." The public information officer said A.A. is simply a microcosm of society.

But like the Boy Scouts of America, the Big Brothers and Big Sisters of America, and the YMCA, Alcoholics Anonymous is a helping organization, designed to reach the vulnerable. While most of A.A.'s members are adults, like the other groups, it also aims to pair newcomers with healthy role models.

Since sexual abuse scandals in nonprofit organizations became public thirty years ago, most of the large youth groups have drafted—and enforce—tough antiabuse policies. They require criminal background checks on volunteers and prohibit one-on-one adult-youth activities. The Boy Scouts, for instance, issued guidelines about inappropriate conduct, which parents must discuss with their children as a condition of joining.

Victor Vieth, a former Minnesota prosecutor who heads the National Child Protection Training Center in Minnesota, has been involved in sexual abuse cases and prevention for twenty-five years. A.A., he told me, is a "ticking time bomb. Like the Catholic Church, like Penn State, and many other groups they have not paid attention to the warning signs," Vieth said.

Because of A.A.'s decentralized structure, though, it takes no responsibility for what happens to the vulnerable women and men who find themselves there, either by court order, an employer's demand, or their own desperate search for help. As Mary C., the GSO's public information officer, wrote in her e-mail to me: "The responsibility for creating a safe environment within the groups rests with the groups themselves and with the individual members.

"Would it be possible for the boards and office to develop some form of document related to vulnerable members?" she continued. "Yes, it is possible, if the members of the fellowship of A.A. in the U.S. and Canada, beginning at the grassroots level of the groups and working its way through the service structure, indicated that they wanted such a piece created."

In April 2012, Richardson posted an accounting of her attempts to attract the local and regional hierarchy's attention on her blog. A writer who claimed to be her district chairman defended A.A.'s handling of her complaints. Richardson's ideas for protecting women, he wrote, would have been "impossible to enforce.

"Our primary purpose is sobriety," he wrote. "At what point do we allow people to date? At one year? Six months? . . . You can't stop people in the rooms from dating; because then you have to decide when they *can* date, and who talks to who— men have to be a year sober to talk to women?" Besides, he noted that two associates in senior positions in his district had ignored those rules themselves and had dated newcomers. "Of course," he wrote, "they aren't going to say anything."

•   •   •

It's been more than two years since Richardson left A.A. for good. She urges her callers to attend Smart Recovery and Secular Organizations for Sobriety, groups she admires. She has also experimented with sips of wine, even allowing herself a glass now and then. "I don't get drunk, and I certainly haven't 'relapsed,'" she says. She says she is "de-programming" herself.

She senses a shifting mood. In 2011, Chris Rock starred as a sexual and financial predator in A.A. in the award-winning Broadway play *The MotherF**ker with the Hat*. The curator of the anti-A.A. blog the *Orange Papers* told me he gets about a million hits each month. Its posts include numerous allegations of sexual abuse within A.A.

Sometimes Richardson agonizes over the years she sacrificed to the group. "My part," she says, "was trusting people in A.A."

7 *Twenty-First-Century Treatment*

Joanna made two big decisions when she turned fifty. The first was that she was going to quit drinking. The second was that she was going to find an evidence-based treatment approach to help her do it.

The director of information technology at a large multistate hospital system, Joanna has an MBA, travels extensively, and is an accomplished mezzo-soprano who learns operas the way others might memorize pop lyrics. For decades, alcohol was an effective tool for squashing anxiety and numbing grief. But over the years, her little issue with chardonnay developed into a big one.

At the end of her drinking career, she was downing almost two liters daily. Her tall, athletic body showed no obvious physical effects, although one time during a gallstone attack, a sonogram revealed a slightly enlarged liver. Terrified, Joanna confessed to her doctor that she drank "a lot of wine" most nights. When her liver enzyme test came back normal, he dismissed her concerns. "You don't have a drinking problem. Your liver's fine! Don't be hard on yourself!" Joanna tolerated her liquor well, rarely appearing inebriated. Then again, she took great pains to conceal it: She threw away most of her big golden bottles, wrapping them first in newspaper and plastic before burying them in the trash can.

Her husband was not so reassuring. One well-oiled evening, Joanna got too loud at a party. "She's a drunk," he said, by way of apologizing to other guests. Joanna's drinking was a frequent source of tension in her marriage, but public humiliation was a blow.

Occasionally, she could stop—during several attempts at in-vitro fertilization, she went cold turkey for weeks, imagining herself as a mother during the shots, blood tests, and ultrasounds. Every time she got the call with the news that the embryos hadn't implanted, her disappointment was somehow tempered by the thought that at least she could drink that night.

When Joanna was in her early forties, her Polish grandmother died, leaving her distraught with grief. She saw a psychiatrist who diagnosed depression and alcohol dependence, and directed her to A.A. Joanna told the doctor that she was disinclined to find an answer to her problems in the twelve steps. Her soft-spoken Canadian mother had tried it several times without success, even staying once for a month in a punitive rehab facility that left her more depressed than ever. To Joanna, the forced attendance at A.A. for all women abusing alcohol was akin to breast cancer before lumpectomies, a limited understanding of the disease prompted the medical community to recommend double mastectomies for every woman with the diagnosis.

Her psychiatrist was unequivocal. Recovery would elude Joanna if she didn't find a sponsor and do the program. "It's the only way," she insisted. So Joanna tried several meetings. She felt most uncomfortable at all-female meetings, where many women imbued their sponsors with a kind of superhuman importance. If the women had good sponsors, they seemed to achieve the status of some sort of omnipotent Boss Mother. If the relationship had soured, the speaker sounded like nothing quite so much as a jilted lover, or an angry, betrayed friend. There seemed to be no room for nuance: Things were either wonderful or awful.

Eventually, Joanna just stopped going—both to the psychiatrist and to meetings. "If A.A. was the only alternative," she says, "I'd rather just drink."

As Joanna neared fifty her mother died, and her stoic Polish-born father, her touchstone, was diagnosed with an aggressive cancer. She tried to moderate her drinking, a wish he had expressed frequently. But as her father neared death, Joanna turned to chardonnay for comfort. "I was drunk when he died," she says, sorrow catching in her voice.

With her consumption up to almost two giant bottles a day, Joanna knew she had to change something—just not the drinking. She took up martial arts. She stopped eating meat and fish. She quit her job of twenty years and founded a new company. Still, she felt sluggish, and in the martial arts class she struggled to concentrate. While Joanna had blamed her job for her drinking, she found herself imbibing even more once she started working from home. Sometimes she'd pour herself a big glass of wine at 2 p.m. and keep drinking all afternoon.

Most days, she woke up with a pounding head and a queasy stomach, and knew she couldn't ignore her drinking problem any longer. She knew she didn't like A.A., and she didn't think the communal approach of Women for Sobriety or other groups would be appropriate, either. So she started researching scientific literature on alcohol treatment.

When her father was sick, she had located the best oncologists for his cancer—doctors familiar with cutting-edge treatments—at a teaching hospital. She applied the same logic to her own condition. "You find someone who studies the most recent journals, someone who's not afraid of new ideas," she says. "I wanted pros."

One evening, Joanna typed the words "non-twelve-step treatment" into Google, and pulled up the website of an alcohol treatment practice in Palos Verdes, California, called Your Empowering Solutions. Its approach relied on cognitive behavioral therapy and motivational interviewing, techniques that help clients avoid triggers and understand the risks of their behavior. Immediately Joanna liked what she read: The psychologists, Mary Ellen Barnes and Ed Wilson, offered an intensive five-day, one-on-one therapy program that enlisted their clients to determine what might work best in stopping their alcohol abuse. She was also intrigued to learn that their clients were overwhelmingly women.

The pair also worked with a family medicine doctor who prescribed naltrexone, a medication that for decades has been effective in blocking alcohol cravings and is used widely in western Europe.

There was no "facility," no lengthy stay, no pottery class,

no equine therapy, no lockdown. Instead, the pair helped clients design a plan for avoiding triggers, develop new interests away from drinking, and learn calming techniques that would replace the need for alcohol's quick fix. The weeklong meetings were followed by twelve or more weeks with regular phone sessions as clients returned to their "real lives."

Barnes and Wilson listed their educational and professional credentials, and conducted the treatment themselves without relying on lesser-trained counselors. Addictions counseling licensing requirements vary widely from state to state, but in many, the most basic certification requires only a high school diploma and 125 hours of addiction studies coursework.

One brisk fall morning, completely hungover, Joanna punched in the numbers on her telephone and Wilson surprised her by answering the line himself. (She was hoping she'd reach an answering service.) She blurted out some questions: What, she asked, would she *do* in their meetings? Wilson told her they would examine the emotional, social, physical, professional, and educational aspects of her life, to see what might need more attention. How did the psychologists define "success"? That, he said, was the outcome she defined for herself, whether it was abstinence, moderating her intake, or simply choosing one option and deciding on the other later. "We don't pretend it's not hard," he told her. "But we don't believe in generalizing that all alcohol abuse is the same. It's a mosaic, with a spectrum, just like any other condition. That's how it is with changing it. We help you find a mosaic that works for you. Everyone's mosaic is different."

Before she lost her nerve, before she even discussed it with her husband, Joanna wrote out a deposit check for twenty-five hundred dollars and drove straight to the post office drop box.

She reserved a room at a luxurious inn near the ocean—Wilson's and Barnes's clients stay in nearby hotels after they are done with their all-day therapy sessions—and booked a flight for mid-November. She didn't want to wait until after the holidays. She wanted to confront her drinking head-on.

•   •   •

The Sunday before her sessions were to start, Joanna ducked into an elegant Southern California Safeway to buy a bottle of her favorite chardonnay—possibly her last—and drove to her hotel. She guzzled it, unpacked, and went to sleep. The next morning, shaking with fear, she climbed the poured pebble steps to Barnes's and Wilson's office. "I couldn't believe I had allowed myself to get to that point," she says.

When she opened the door, Barnes's elderly dog, Shogun, loped up to greet her. Barnes, a California native with thick copper curls, a gentle voice, and a direct gaze, stands as a foil for the towering, mustachioed Wilson, who, despite forty years away from his native Pennsylvania, sometimes sounds as if he is still there. ("Water" comes out like "wooder.") Wilson sometimes uses the vernacular of his past as a steelworker and commercial fisherman. He rolls up his shirtsleeves, not bothering to conceal the giant black koi tattoo that meanders down his left forearm. When he laughs, which is often, he flashes a gold front tooth etched with a tiny star. When Joanna first noticed it, she felt herself relax. "Suddenly he seemed a lot less threatening," she says.

Joanna took a seat in a comfortable leather chair and answered some simple questions. Was her hotel okay? Did she have health, social, marital concerns? What were her hopes for a life without alcohol abuse? There were no inquiries about her childhood, or unresolved feelings about her mother. The questions were straightforward, and focused on her vision for the present and the future—not the past. Joanna wrote out a check for the remainder of the total: $8,750 for the five days of therapy, a medical evaluation, and three months of follow-up sessions—even daily if necessary. It's a bargain by the standards of private rehab. Other clinics nearby charge upward of a thousand dollars a day for a minimum twenty-eight-day stay.

As Joanna looked through her paperwork, she noticed another unusual document requiring her signature. It said she understood that all records of her visit would be destroyed after she left. Substance abuse treatment programs that accept medical insurance or local, state, or federal funding typically keep records of each patient. Under some circumstances, such records can be made available to any government agency, prospective employer, and insurance company. This fact alone makes many people reluctant to seek treatment, since exposure can have devastating personal and career consequences.

•   •   •

The morning of their first meeting, Wilson drove Joanna to the office of Dr. Tim Norcross, a family medicine doctor who conducts thorough physical exams of the pair's clients. If the client is in good health (those needing detox are referred first to hospitals), he prescribes naltrexone, a drug developed in the United States in 1963 and long used in western Europe to treat alcohol and drug dependence. The World Health Organization approved the use of the drug in 1994, followed by the Food and Drug Administration in 1995 and the American Medical Association in 1996. But few Americans—either laymen or physicians—are familiar with it. It is available in generic pill form for around a hundred dollars a month, so pharmaceutical companies don't do much to promote it.

Naltrexone works by blocking the brain's release of endorphins, chemicals that allow humans to feel pleasure during sex, after exercise, or when they take some drugs, such as alcohol. When this interaction is blocked, drinkers feel less compulsion to drink. Without a reward, there is less desire. Naltrexone also allows the brain to jump-start a normal production and release of endorphins, which helps to suppress the craving to drink. This two-pronged approach—cutting the cravings and blocking the rewards—helps people moderate their alcohol use. (Because it targets opioid receptors, not the release of endorphins, it does not affect or diminish pleasure from exercise or sex.)

Unlike disulfiram, another medicine that is often used to treat alcohol abuse, naltrexone does not make you feel sick if you drink alcohol while taking it. After publication of the first two randomized, controlled trials in 1992, dozens of studies have confirmed its efficacy in reducing frequency and severity of drinking. In 2006, the NIAAA released the results of the three-year study of nearly fourteen hundred subjects that examined which combinations of pharmaceutical treatments and behavioral therapies might best treat alcohol dependence. Subjects of the study (known by its acronym, COMBINE) were enrolled in one of nine protocols, which used different variations of drugs, placebos, behavior therapy, and what is known as medical management—supervising, educating, monitoring, and caring for a patient. Naltrexone, when combined with medical management, was found to be the most effective of all treatments.

Two other drugs, acamprosate and topiramate, have also shown limited promise for treating alcohol abuse in several studies. The FDA approved acamprosate, used extensively in Europe, for the treatment of alcohol abuse in 2004; researchers have found that it improved rates of continuous abstinence, percent of days abstinent, and the time until the first drink. Topiramate, an anticonvulsant, has similar effects.

Dozens of studies show that naltrexone and topiramate reduce the number of drinking days among those who desire moderation, and increase the ability for others to stay abstinent. In repeated clinical trials, naltrexone has been found to reduce the percentage of heavy drinking days and the number of drinks consumed. Meta-analyses have shown that oral naltrexone is effective in preventing relapse to heavy drinking— or any drinking at all. In a study of the use of extended-release naltrexone, Yale researcher Stephanie O'Malley found that 32 percent of patients receiving extended-release naltrexone, which is delivered by injection and therefore eliminates the need for patients to take it every day, were abstinent over six months, compared with 11 percent using a placebo. That is nearly a 200 percent difference.

Only a handful of studies, published in the last five years or so, have even considered analyzing the effects of gender on the drug. But some small studies have reported that naltrexone reduces alcohol euphoria most effectively in women, as well as people carrying a variant of the OPRM1 gene, an opioid receptor gene that plays a key role in both pain perception and addiction. Different variants of the gene may help explain differences in the way humans respond to alcohol, as well as how effectively the drug binds to the opioid receptor. Researchers are hopeful that more widespread clinical testing can yield clues about which patients will respond best. For example, in 2011, Canadian researchers found that among those with a variant of the gene, known as A118G, 87 percent were able to reduce their drinking days significantly. That compared to 49 percent of those receiving placebos, and 55 percent without the gene but who received either the drug or a placebo.

Studies involving naltrexone and gene variants have been small, using only a few hundred subjects, but researchers are optimistic that the findings can be used to help identify which people are best suited for the drug. The Canadian researchers, who studied twenty women and twenty men, wrote that they were optimistic that their findings might help in the search for personalized alcohol treatment.

Another study showed promising signs for naltrexone's use for women. In 2008, Brown University scientists examined naltrexone's effects on 180 heavy drinkers, of whom seventy-two were women. The study was notable because the subjects were not seeking treatment for their drinking—they had simply answered a research ad placed in newspapers. It was also significant because the subjects recorded their cravings, consumption, and moods after drinking on handheld devices that allowed the researchers to analyze data in real time from home—not memories recorded later, or in the clinical setting of a lab. In that study, the researchers found that naltrexone was effective in reducing the quantity of alcohol and frequency of alcohol consumption, but they noted some important differences: It significantly blunted alcohol's euphoric effects on women.

In the United States, naltrexone is generally prescribed with the goal of at least temporary abstinence, allowing patients to break their dangerous cycles of drinking before attempting moderation at a later date. In Finland, however, an American doctor named John David Sinclair uses it for heavy drinkers who plan to drink for the rest of their lives. His theory is this: If you drink, prompting the brain to release endorphins, each glass of wine reinforces that behavior. But if you drink and get no endorphin release, the urge fades. With the craving blocked, problem drinkers are able to limit their consumption—not by abstaining, but by drinking a moderate amount. Using this method, Sinclair claims a success rate of 78 percent, using as a yardstick the practice of drinking within safe limits (although those vary from country to country).

Sinclair advises his patients to take the pill an hour or so before drinking. With the drug, heavy drinking will give way to normal drinking. Naltrexone itself is "lapse prevention," but the method demands compliance in order to work.

This approach is rarely embraced in the United States, since it requires little behavioral adjustment on the part of the client. And even Wilson, a fan of the drug, says it's no magical answer. But he says it helps to prepare a problem drinker for a new kind of life. "Think about it: Less drinking tends to free up time for other activities, and a lot of clients find themselves easing out of alcohol abuse the same way they fell into it."

* * *

Joanna wasn't looking for magic, though; she was looking for results. When she stepped into Tim Norcross's bright, modern office, the staff was welcoming and friendly, and even the magazines were upbeat. When she fretted about her weight, his kind nurse told her to step on the scale backward. When she worried aloud to Norcross that she had ruined her liver

forever—a fear she had harbored since her mother's days in
A.A.—he told her, "Let's find out, and move forward." Indeed, while most injured organs can heal, new tissue appears
in the form of scars. The liver, however, is able to replace damaged tissue with new cells. Despite her years of heavy drinking, Joanna's liver enzymes were normal. "I dodged a bullet,
and I know it," she says.

Norcross prescribed a week's worth of the antianxiety
medication Klonopin, as well as three months of naltrexone.
Research shows that taking the drug for three to six months
gives new, nondrinking behaviors time to establish themselves
into patterns. Joanna returned to Barnes's and Wilson's office.

Then the three went out to lunch, to a local Tex-Mex
restaurant known for its generous salads. There was no dining
hall, no other patients she had to make small talk with: just
Joanna and her two shrinks.

The next step in Joanna's treatment was a written test designed to evaluate her emotional maturity, a series of sentence
stems that she had to complete. Such tests have been in use
since the late nineteenth century as a tool to assess attitudes,
beliefs, and motivation. Wilson administers one designed in
the 1970s by Jane Loevinger, a developmental psychologist
who taught at Washington University in St. Louis. Loevinger
was a pioneer in the study of female psychology, as well as
the concept of ego development. She theorized that humans
advance through a series of stages that reflect growing levels
of cognitive and emotional maturity, and that they make decisions based on their gradual internalization of social rules and
personal experiences.

Her test, known as the Washington University Sentence
Completion Test, measures nine stages, and is used as a tool in

settings as varied as freshman dorms and corporate recruitment. It seeks to assess how a person's experiences and identity — their hardwired selves — shape their approach to life.

Joanna found the exercise amusing, and raced through it in about a half hour. Wilson, who has scored thousands of the tests for medical schools, prisons, and elite branches of the military, tallied her score as an 8, a stage Loevinger described as "autonomous." Joanna's answers to the brief sentence stems, such as "A man's job . . ." and "When I'm criticized . . ." revealed a highly evolved sense of independence and self. (Loevinger found that the majority of American adults tend to settle in stage 5, which she called "self-aware." At this stage, adults have limited curiosity about the experiences of others. Their powerful motivators are guilt and concerns about what others might think.)

The test, they say, offers valuable clues for how to shape a client's treatment. Those who score at the higher end of the scale tend to be independent thinkers who are introspective and aware of their inner conflicts. They are able to tolerate, even appreciate, life's ambiguities, paradoxes, and inconsistencies and can integrate new experiences, learning, and skills into changing self-perceptions.

Those who score in the middle ranges often have fixed self-perceptions, tend to prize conformity, and function best within strict rubrics. Wilson says such people are better suited to A.A., with its clearly delineated rules and limits. Many find comfort in the repetitive axioms of A.A. ("Once an alcoholic, always an alcoholic") and its sobriety chips. Those who score higher on Loevinger's test tend to do least well with twelve-step programs. "A.A. is not for people who have a lot of questions," Wilson says.

As they continued through the week, Wilson and Barnes addressed Joanna's goals for her future, examined what prompted her drinking, and discussed ideas she might have for achieving better physical and mental health. That task seemed overwhelming, but as she wrote out her objectives, she realized that her leisure time could be productive instead of numbing. Her aspirations were far from lofty: In addition to adding more exercise and eating better, she wanted to finish decorating her master bedroom, organize her belongings better, and hang pictures that had been sidelined next to the wall for years.

In the afternoons after her sessions, Joanna took long walks on the beach and listened to meditation CDs. Skeptical at first, she was surprised at how they were able to help relieve her anxiety in a way completely different from alcohol. As she returned to Pennsylvania, she felt armed with knowledge—about herself, her personal development, and the vision she had for her life.

Given Joanna's drinking history, Barnes warned her outright that she would not be a good candidate for moderation, even with naltrexone. At first, Joanna was disappointed. "You mean I really can't drink again?" she said. "You can try it," Barnes said, "but I would wait for at least a year."

Back home, Joanna took naltrexone for ninety days, stopping when she began suffering from headaches (they are among the drug's side effects). But by then, she says, she had developed a routine of work, healthy eating, voracious evening reading—when she was drinking, she was always too inebriated to remember where she had left off—and a rededication to exercise. She made a weekly schedule for yoga and jogging, and stepped up her participation in martial arts. (Since quitting drinking, she has advanced four belt colors.) Quickly, she says, she began to see the possibilities for a better life. She was also surprised to feel her desire for chardonnay fade, so much so that she didn't feel the need to remove the bottles from her pantry. "I still have some, for guests," she says. "My husband could take or leave it, and if people come over and want some, they can."

Her transition was surprisingly smooth. What she had dreaded for so long—shifting from a drinking life to a non-drinking one—had so many pleasant side effects, she doesn't even feel tempted to slip. "I wanted to live my life without drinking the way I had been, and I was really focused on that. Drinking would only take me back a step, and I knew it." For example, fights in her marriage often centered on her drinking, but drinking, of course, was easy to blame. Without the veil of alcohol, she and her husband communicate more directly about what might be bothering them.

That is not to say that there have been no stumbling blocks. Several months into her wine-free life, the neighbors at her summer lake house invited her to an evening barbecue. At previous gatherings, Joanna drank too much, but then again, so did almost everybody else. On one hand, she didn't want to feel uncomfortable, sipping soda while everyone else got sloshed; on the other, she didn't want to have to out herself in a small community. She took a deep breath and told her neighbor the truth: She was new to not drinking, and was unsure about whether to attend. Her neighbor was silent. Finally, she said, "Then maybe it's better if you don't come."

Joanna hung up the phone and sobbed.

A few months later, when I met Joanna for the first time at her house, she was anxious about a long-planned weekend with her best friends from college. They were scheduled to gather in Chicago to eat in the newest restaurants, see an exhibit at the Art Institute, and shop. She was worried, since girls' weekends often include copious amounts of alcohol. Joanna had told them all ahead of time that she wouldn't be imbibing with them, but they encouraged her to come.

Joanna was delayed and arrived in Chicago long past the scheduled meeting time. Once she made it to the restaurant to meet her friends, she noticed they had already had a few cocktails each. Anxious at first, Joanna downed her seltzer with lime. Their buzzes fading, they ordered dinner—and talked deep into the night. Joanna was thrilled in the morning: She remembered everything everybody had said, and didn't have to repeat questions or cover up for her herself by saying, "Oh, yes, that's right, you told me that!"

When she travels to the Caribbean each January, she has to swallow hard when she hears the steel drums play, and sees couples downing frosty rum drinks on the beach. "It's a chain reaction, and I understand it," she says. "I hear the music, smell the saltwater, and want a drink like everybody else." In the beginning, she dreaded occasions where wine had been her crutch—the first boating excursion of the summer, for example—without a tumbler of wine. She would call Barnes. "What if someone says something?" Joanna asked. "Nobody cares about your drinking," Barnes told her, "as long as you are not interfering with theirs."

A few months ago, she and her husband went to the opera in Manhattan. It was her first without chardonnay. Joanna knew the libretto—this was *Carmen,* one of her favorites—and as she took her seat she felt her pulse quicken. The curtains rose, and the singer's notes were so pure and electric, Joanna felt as if they were entering her bloodstream. As she followed the opera, she, too, felt the gigantic emotions—jealousy, rage, passion, joy. Now, the extravagance of her enjoyment felt as amplified as the music itself.

•   •   •

Like Joanna, Wilson's and Barnes's clients tend to be educated and highly motivated women. Six years into their partnership, their 240 clients report a 70 percent success rate. This means that clients say they have achieved the outcome they desire, whether it is abstaining or moderating. Of the remaining 30 percent, half drop out, and the other 15 percent continue to struggle.

Many battle with identity crises that crop up in middle age. Alcohol might seem like the culprit, but it is often more likely the symptom of a larger problem. "They might feel powerless over alcohol, but the real problem is that they feel powerless in their marriages, in their jobs, in their decisions," says Barnes. Many women had established careers before they had children, then chose to stay home. "They might have their first baby in their late thirties or early forties and decide that after all this dedication at work, they'll stay home with the baby," she says. "It's not that they don't love their babies, but they didn't count on what they were giving up. They're not getting a pat on the back for a job well done—the baby's crying. They're not getting paid. They're bored—and really anxious, and feel guilty that they are bored and anxious."

So they drink to get through it—and before they know it, fifteen years have passed. "Alcohol works," says Barnes, "until it doesn't."

Barnes and Wilson describe a recent client, a former

businesswoman who left her job after the birth of her second child. As a way to keep busy, she had hosted occasional jewelry parties. The more wine drunk, the more jewelry sold. One morning after, her head pounding, she surveyed her empties—thirty-five bottles of chardonnay for twenty women—and called Barnes and Wilson for an appointment.

For many such clients, their advice (and they give it freely) is straightforward. If stay-at-home mothers complain that they're bored, they suggest finding work they find more meaningful. If women are overwhelmed with the tasks of modern motherhood, Barnes and Wilson point out other solutions: cutting back on their kids' extracurricular activities and having them pitch in more—making their own lunches, doing their own laundry. Most emphatically, they prescribe finding alternative activities in the late afternoon or evening that have nothing to do with alcohol—volunteering at Habitat for Humanity; taking a yoga class; joining Audubon Society bird walks; going for a long stroll with the dog.

If clients feel trapped in unfulfilling marriages, the counselors are likely to suggest recalibrating the relationship. One of their most common findings is about how frequently drinking spouses are afraid to be assertive in their personal relationships, regardless of how they act professionally. Many female clients feel resentful about the sacrifices they made to raise children, and are also envious of their spouses' success. They turn to alcohol rather than make an affirmative change in their professional or personal status.

Unlike in most treatment programs, Barnes and Wilson also incorporate the client's significant other into the sessions. "Alcohol abuse doesn't occur in a vacuum," Wilson says.

They also discuss a woman's diet and exercise habits, as

well as her hormone levels. As hormones fluctuate in meno-pause, alcohol can intensify symptoms such as hot flashes and insomnia. Drinking even moderate amounts of alcohol can raise estrogen levels, and many studies have linked it to an in-creased risk of breast cancer.

Many of their clients are thin, preferring to drink, rather than eat, their calories. Often, they are also dedicated exercis-ers, a paradox confirmed in a recent study that found that the more some people drink, the more they exercise. They point out that alcohol cravings are often triggered by hunger, not a desire to get high. Calorie counters, concerned with stay-ing thin, may forgo balanced meals for more booze—and then exercise to keep from gaining. Though it may seem obvious, Wilson and Barnes suggest drawing out meal plans that in-clude plenty of protein, fruit, and vegetables.

They also emphasize the importance of learning to cope with the aftermath of an occasional drink or two. If clients drink while they are trying to abstain, they encourage them to call. "It's not, 'Oh my God, you've *relapsed*,'" Barnes says. "We point out how well they did on so many of the other days before it. You had a drink; it's not the end of the world. You didn't 'ruin your sobriety' or 'undo' anything."

She likens the concept of "relapse"—it's a term she and Wilson avoid—to a pattern that is common among dieters. "Let's say that over the course of six months, you've lost twenty-two pounds by changing your diet and exercising more," she says. "Are you back to square one if you gain five back in the month of December? Certainly not," she says. "You return to your healthy habits, and lay off the pecan pie and the Christmas cookies."

Recently, a woman who once drank two bottles of pinot

grigio a day called Barnes in a panic. It had been a year since they'd spoken, and more than two years since she had left treatment.

"I went out for lunch with my girlfriend and had a glass of wine," the woman blurted.

"Okay," said Barnes. "Did you go home and continue drinking?"

"No," the woman said.

"Did you drink too much the day after?"

"No."

"I'm not sure I'm understanding," Barnes said.

"I relapsed! I drank!" the woman said, near tears.

"Let's get this straight," Barnes said. "When we met you drank two bottles of wine a day. You decided to change that habit, and you did. The other day you had a glass of wine with your girlfriend. One glass. This is not a 'relapse.' This is success."

When clients face challenging situations—weddings, parties, conventions—Wilson and Barnes encourage their clients to call for support with ideas about how to avoid falling into familiar patterns, no matter how long ago they wrapped up their sessions. They also suggest keeping a few doses of naltrexone around for a few years, in order to discourage binges.

· · ·

Not everyone can drink in moderation. Most experts agree that some people, for whatever reason—a genetic vulnerability, as well as a combination of environmental, psychological, and physical factors—cannot drink in a controlled way.

"But that is a very, very small group of people," Barnes

says. "Like so many other conditions, from asthma to eating disorders, there is a huge continuum for alcohol abuse."

It is not always easy to convince clients what conventional wisdom has held dear for the past eighty years—telling a woman she is not an alcoholic, and doesn't have to call herself one, seems almost as radical as hearing your mother tell you to ditch the sunscreen before heading to the beach. How to shift the way we understand alcohol and how to manage it for a varied population—and especially for women—will require some effort.

Since it was released in 2006, the COMBINE study appears to have made few inroads. Tim Norcross, the family doctor who treats Wilson's and Barnes's clients, had never heard of naltrexone when the psychologists approached him about working together in 2007—and he was just a few years out of medical school.

He wonders why nicotine addiction—which has been treated for twenty-five years with medicine—has such a different reputation. Ex-smokers don't call themselves "recovering smokers," and ads for Chantix, which blocks nicotine receptors so that smoking or chewing the drug can't activate them, fill medical journals. Anyone over eighteen can buy nicotine gum at the drugstore.

•   •   •

Barnes's and Wilson's program incorporates a number of methods that have been scientifically proven to reduce alcohol abuse, and they are among a growing number of practitioners who rely on science to treat their patients. I focused on Joanna because she was representative of the numerous women I've spoken to who were aware of the drawbacks of twelve-step treatment, and had researched an alternative approach that would be tailored to her. The last I spoke with her, in January 2013, she was happy, not drinking, and reported feeling healthier than she'd ever been.

In fact, there are many alternatives to Alcoholics Anonymous, including a group called Smart Recovery, which is a secular nonprofit organization that employs motivational and cognitive behavioral therapy in meetings and online support groups. Another organization, Rational Recovery, offers tools for alcohol and other substance abusers to recognize their own "addictive voice," and find abstinence on their own. It has no groups or meetings because it believes such gatherings merely reinforce the notion of a crippling lifelong disease. SOS, Secular Organizations for Sobriety, is a network of autonomous, nonprofessional, science-based recovery groups.

Mark Willenbring, psychiatrist and former director of treatment research at the NIAAA, sees patients in private practice in Minneapolis. He has developed a new company, ALLTYR, which is dedicated to providing scientifically based treatment, and educating the public about twenty-first-century approaches to alcohol and drug abuse. Like Barnes and Wilson, he treats patients with individualized, personal therapy in his office for a fraction of the cost of rehab. "As taxpayers, as insurance policyholders, and insurance companies themselves," he says, "we're wasting tremendous amounts of money, and not getting anything out of what we spend. It just doesn't have to be this way."

Dee-Dee Stout, a California addictions counselor, agrees. In 2011, Stout cofounded AA2.org, an online self-help website that guides clients through evidence-based methods of recovery. Stout, the author of *Coming to Harm Reduction Kicking and Screaming: Looking for Harm Reduction in a 12-Step World,* travels globally to lecture on various approaches to alcohol abuse, including harm reduction. The concept brings together two seemingly opposite ideas: that people can be in recovery and yet continue to use substances responsibly. Ken Anderson, a community organizer in Brooklyn, formed a group called HAMS, a peer-led support group that offers guidance on harm reduction, abstinence, and moderation.

Stanton Peele, a New Jersey psychologist, lawyer, and author of nine books, has argued for decades that moderation is an acceptable goal for many problem drinkers. Peele is past the usual American retirement age, but for him slowing down is out of the question. As a lecturer, his message has never been in more demand, and his third and especially provocative book, *The Diseasing of America: How We Allowed Recovery Zealots and the Treatment Industry to Convince Us We Are Out of Control,* continues to get new online reviews more than twenty years after its publication.

The debate about abstinence rages on, however. Consider the case of Audrey Kishline, a problem drinker who struggled with A.A.'s concepts, and in 1994 founded an organization called Moderation Management for nondependent problem drinkers to help maintain moderate alcohol use. The group says its approach doesn't suit all problem drinkers, and that abstinence is best for some.

In January 2000, Kishline posted a message saying that moderation didn't work for her, and that she would begin attending A.A. and other abstinence-based groups. Two months later, having returned to A.A., Kishline had a blood-alcohol content of more than three times the legal limit; Kishline sped the wrong way on an icy highway in Washington State, killing a thirty-eight-year-old man and his twelve-year-old daughter. She served three and a half years of a four-and-a-half-year sentence.

This tragic accident has been used as irrefutable proof that for all problem drinkers, moderation is dangerous—and impossible.

Peele and others say that a single anecdote shouldn't decide treatments for large populations. The ultimate goal is an array of approaches for the array of patients.

Willenbring looks forward to the day when Americans view alcohol problems like they now see depression. Forty years ago, those who suffered from it had few choices. They could wait in agony for the hemorrhaging of tears to cease, the anxiety to dissipate. Families committed desperate patients— typically after suicide attempts—to psychiatric hospitals, where treatments were dubious and scary: around-the-clock sedation, isolation, and the full-scale seizures brought on by electroconvulsive therapy administered without anesthesia.

Since the advent of Prozac and its descendants, depression is part of the national conversation—and often a topic patients discuss with their primary-care doctors. In fact, the number of Americans treated with antidepressants between 1996 and 2007 went from 13.3 million to 27 million, according to a study of national mental health surveys. Of those patients, more than half were prescribed the drug by their primary-care doctors.

By contrast, Willenbring says, fewer than 10 percent of the twenty million Americans who suffer from an alcohol abuse disorder ever get specialized treatment for it—and that's usually only after they've suffered a serious physical or social consequence. Every week, Willenbring talks to female patients whose doctors refuse to prescribe medications that can help curb alcohol cravings. "They get referred to A.A., or rehab," he says.

"When a patient has high cholesterol, you don't wait for her to have a heart attack before you prescribe statins and make some dietary changes," he says. "When a patient has mild asthma, you prescribe an inhaler. You don't wait until he can't breathe and then ship him off to the ICU. You intervene when the condition is mild."

He suggests that those who are concerned about their drinking seek evidence-based intervention if they can answer yes to the following three questions. "Do you set limits and repeatedly go over them? Do you have a persistent desire to quit or cut down and are unable to do it? Do you have frequent physical consequences, such as nausea or headaches, after time spent drinking?"

Yet fifty years after Jellinek distanced himself from the drinker's curve, conventional thinking about alcohol still retains its concepts. It's hard to imagine a realm of medicine in which the gap between science and practice is so great.

Change will take some doing. One useful step, Willenbring says, would be to distinguish more clearly between "at-risk drinking" and "alcohol dependence." At-risk drinking is drinking more than is medically advisable, and puts heavier drinkers at risk for developing an alcohol-use disorder. Alcohol dependence has a number of specific diagnostic criteria and professionals need to learn how to identify it. It's not clear that they do. Primary-care doctors do not always pick up on the signs of alcohol abuse until blood tests reveal a damaged liver. If medical schools want to train a generation of doctors who can handle this problem, they need to do more than shuffle their students off to meetings in church basements to learn about addiction. They need to teach doctors how to screen for and counsel at-risk drinkers and to treat patients with alcohol-use disorders medically.

Rather than entrust recovering drinkers as the first and last mechanism of support, we need to convince insurance companies and federal insurance programs to reimburse doctors for their new role, and patients for expensive medication. The injectable form of naltrexone is the priciest—up to a thousand dollars a shot—but compared to rehab, it's cost effective even when it's combined with medical monitoring. When women learn that they can manage their drinking without the stigma, cost, and time of inpatient rehab, they might be willing to ask for help sooner.

•   •   •

If women need more reason to question the one-size-fits-all approach to alcohol abuse, they need only look at a map of the world. No one seems to agree, for one thing, on what the healthy daily dose of alcohol should be. From Sweden to Australia, Denmark to South Africa, drinking recommendations for women are twice the amount health officials suggest for American women. In Spain, Italy, and France, where wine is a revered national birthright, the suggested limits are even higher. Women in those countries live the longest of any other country in Europe, dying at around eighty-four. On the Greek island of Ikaria, which has one of the world's largest concentration of centenarians, wine consumption for both men and women is between two and four glasses a day. Of course, many women in these countries—particularly those in Greece—share a healthy diet that is rich in fish, olive oil, legumes, and greens.

And the manner of consumption is expected to be different, too. In Spain, for example, the recommendation for women is to consume no more than thirty grams of ethyl alcohol (roughly three five-ounce glasses of wine) a day. This converts to a glass of wine at lunch, an aperitif with a snack, and a glass of wine at dinner. Having food—especially proteins, fats, and dense carbohydrates—slows down the absorption of alcohol into the bloodstream, giving the liver more time to process it.

In the United States, health officials suggest one drink a day for women, two for men. For women, heavy or "at-risk" drinking is anything more than three drinks in one day, or seven in one week. (For men, that figure is four drinks a day, or fourteen a week.) I'm not implying causation, but it's interesting to note that American women die sooner than their European counterparts. Hispanic women live the longest, until an average of eighty-two; white women, to an average of eighty-one; and black women, to an average of seventy-seven.

There are a number of reasons the U.S. recommendations are so low. According to Dr. Raul Caetano, dean of the School of Health Professions at the University of Texas Southwestern Medical School, in the United States and in northern Europe, people are aware that heavy drinking is not considered respectable. In these cultures especially, people naturally underreport their consumption. "Some people might forget or simply not know," he said during a phone interview. "But others underreport because they don't want to reveal how much they drink."

Some northern European studies show that there is a 50 percent difference between what people buy, Caetano says, and what they admit to actually drinking. So unless people are storing up their wine and vodka for Armageddon, chances are they shave off a few drinks.

I asked Dr. Caetano whether researchers in those countries would compensate for that by suggesting people drink less.

He answered the question indirectly: In cultures where alcohol has been integrated for millennia, health officials have a higher tolerance for its associated risks. Guidelines are also calculated according to what a nation considers a serious problem. For example, in the United States, where fifteen out of a hundred thousand deaths are in automobile accidents, researchers might be hoping to reduce the risk from alcohol-related car crashes. In the Netherlands, where auto deaths are rare, public health officials might be more concerned with preventing liver disease.

Fred Rotgers, a New Jersey clinical psychologist who is a pioneer in harm reduction and a cofounder of the online self-help group AA2.org, says there are also political motivations. Amid the "war on drugs," scientists who receive federal funding for alcohol research are unlikely to take liberal attitudes toward any aspect of substance use, he says. "You have legislators who view all alcohol consumption as morally wrong," he says. "They're not considering that the vast majority of people who consume alcohol do so responsibly. But if that's who controls your grant money, you've got to be careful." According to the Pew Research Center, about 27 percent of the 113th Congress belonged to religious groups that prohibit alcohol.

Many researchers agree that the restraint of U.S. guidelines stems in part from the many studies that suggest a link between breast cancer and even moderate alcohol consumption. As I was finishing my reporting for this book, another study showed an association. It was a worry that haunted many of my sources, and multitudes of my moderate-drinking friends.

On one hand, moderate alcohol consumption has been associated with lower rates of heart disease and stroke, certain types of cancers, dementia, and diabetes.

Yet a 2011 study of 106,000 women in the *Journal of the American Medical Association* found that women who drank between three and six drinks a week were about 15 percent more likely than nondrinkers to be diagnosed with breast cancer. Among women had two drinks a day, the risk rose to 51 percent. It made no difference whether the women drank wine, beer, or spirits.

The alarming percentage numbers were reported widely in the popular press, often without noting that, in fact, they translated to small increases in small numbers. But Dr. Steven A. Narod, a breast cancer scientist at the Women's College Research Institute in Toronto, noted in an accompanying *JAMA* editorial that, according to the data, women who routinely have a drink a day could expect their ten-year risk of breast cancer to increase from 2.8 percent to 3.5 percent. For women who have two drinks a day, that risk would rise from 2.8 percent to 4.1 percent. The numbers were adjusted for age, family history of the disease, smoking, and weight.

The study, led by Dr. Wendy Chen, an assistant professor of medicine at Harvard Medical School, analyzed lifelong consumption patterns of nearly 106,000 predominantly white nurses ages 30 to 55 between 1980 and 2008. They found that drinking both early in adult life and after age forty was associated with higher risk. The authors said that although the exact mechanism isn't known, it may involve alcohol's effects on a woman's estrogen levels. There is evidence that alcohol increases a woman's blood level of estrogen, and high levels of estrogen are a known risk factor for breast cancer.

Like many similar studies on alcohol's risks, the *JAMA* study was based on self-reports, which are not always reliable. It lacked a control group and also found no evidence that giving up drinking lowers a woman's risk of breast cancer.

What's a wine lover to do? Experts cautioned against overreacting to the findings. Even Chen said women should weigh the risks and benefits of wine to prevent cardiovascular disease.

Dr. Lisa Schwartz, a professor of community and family medicine at Dartmouth Medical School, is skeptical of observed epidemiological studies, which she says share "an important weakness." While this study asked questions about drinking habits, Schwartz says, other factors might explain the findings. "We need to be humble about what observational studies tell us, since we can't randomly control for what we've observed."

In an editorial she cowrote for the *Journal of the National Cancer Institute,* Schwartz cited 2009 reports in the popular media warning women that a drink a day could raise their risk of breast cancer. But the coverage, based on a study published in the *JNCI*, didn't mention the magnitude of the risk. The researchers compared breast cancer rates among women who drank more than fifteen drinks a week to women who drank one or two drinks a week. The investigators observed a 0.6 percent increase in the risk of breast cancer diagnosis, from 2 percent to 2.6 percent. That's a tiny fraction of an increase, but it represents a 30 percent jump—and that's the figure that got reported.

Schwartz points out that the women who drink alcohol might be more health conscious, drinking one glass of wine a day for cardiovascular health. It's possible that those women are more likely to get more regular mammograms. "Maybe it's more screening that explains the higher breast cancer diagnosis—not the alcohol," Schwartz says. "To read the reports and even the press releases from the journals themselves, you're led to believe that every drink makes a difference. That's just not what the data show," she says. "That's dramatically overstating the risks."

Such reports instill at once too much fear and too much hope: "There's inherent tension between wanting to tell people what might help them stay healthy versus being far too definitive and ramping up fear with things we're not sure about. I've never seen a randomized trial of high-risk women changing their habits and therefore being less likely to be diagnosed with breast cancer," she says. "This isn't like lung cancer and smoking."

The best approach, Schwartz says, is for researchers to be honest and say, "'We're really not sure, but with alcohol, at least, the risk is very small.'"

Some studies have shown that the nutrient folate, found in oranges, fortified grains, and green leafy vegetables, might protect against the increased risk of breast cancer associated with alcohol consumption because alcohol can reduce the cancer-protecting folate in the bloodstream. Scientists think that folate may be involved in how cells activate certain genes, and that low levels of folate can alter chemicals that affect DNA. This in turn might alter a cell's ability to repair itself, or divide incorrectly, and become cancerous.

Risk, after all, isn't destiny. Getting a flu shot lowers your risk of getting the flu, but it doesn't guarantee it. Exercising doesn't guarantee that you won't get heart disease, but it lowers the odds. Not drinking isn't going to prevent you from getting breast cancer, but it may lower your risk for developing certain kinds of it.

"Women need to be aware of the numbers," Schwartz says, "and decide for themselves."

Conclusion

American women's relationship with alcohol offers a fascinating window on how far we've come—and how far we haven't. The fact that we drink to excess far more often than our mothers is proof that we have passed a dubious milestone. Forget about boys will be boys. These days, many women have taken advantage of modern equality to behave just as stupidly as men at bachelorette parties, sporting events, and girls' nights out.

As with men's excesses, all this carousing may have benefits. In a few decades, maybe America's captains of industry will be drawn from members of the Old Girls Network who forged lifelong bonds overdoing it at sorority parties. After all, generations of men who dominated politics and business came of age as drinking buddies. But as a plethora of scientific studies have demonstrated in recent years, women *are* different. When they match men beer for beer, they get drunk quicker. And when they end up in an A.A.-driven rehab, their needs are different. It's why so many women I interviewed felt that their trip to twelve-step treatment was a journey to a foreign land where they didn't speak the language or understand the local customs.

After years of speaking to women who have tried to cope with their drinking, a few simple findings emerge.

We need to take advantage of twenty-first-century science. We've learned a lot about how the brain works since the founding of A.A. in 1935. And we need to acknowledge what nearly every research study has found in recent years: One size could not possibly fit all. If alcoholism really is a medical condition—and there's plenty of evidence that addiction has a genetic component—then we should not blame the patient for failing to "work the program" when one type of treatment fails. We don't ask cancer patients to explain their "part" in a course of chemotherapy that didn't achieve the desired result.

For some, these words are heresy. Any questioning of the twelve-step dogma, they argue, threatens the lives of those who have tamed an otherwise intractable problem. That, of course, is not my intent. Women who have achieved success with A.A. or other twelve-step approaches should consider themselves lucky and keep attending meetings. But for those for whom it doesn't work—and that's the vast majority of people who try it—it's worth searching for other answers.

We can't know all the reasons women are drinking more, and by no means do I mean to suggest that it's the fault of women's progress in our society. Feminism is about gaining power, but when you take people out of one milieu and drop them in another, it changes them in unpredictable ways. Some

thrive. Others struggle. So it is with women in the postmodern universe. It's not that the trip there was a mistake, it's that the side effects need to be treated appropriately.

We consider alcohol a social equalizer, but we haven't been paying attention to the disparity of consequences. Women get drunk faster, and they suffer health problems from excess drinking faster, too.

Rather than spend resources after women have "hit bottom" like a group of midcentury white guys, we need to educate ourselves, our doctors, and our legal system about new approaches—ones that have nothing to do with surrendering control. That's something women have been experts in since the two genders began negotiating power.

Women are drinking more because they can. They have the means, and the freedom, to do it—and the stress that makes them feel they need to. They've provided a growth market for wine and spirits manufacturers in the United States, and are a bright spot for alcohol producers and importers in emerging economies from India to China, where women have typically drunk less than men. Indeed, in Uganda, the number of young women who identify themselves as "new drinkers" has edged out young men. Advertisers have taken note: In neighboring Tanzania, a beer ad shows a young couple marching down the aisle toward the altar. The groom reaches into his pocket for the bride's wedding ring, but can't find it. The bride's father glares, and the bride is disgusted. Then the beer's mascot, an animated leopard, appears out of nowhere with the glittering gold band. The bride reaches for the ring, elated, and joins the leopard in a beer-fueled wedding dance. The message is clear: Marriage will let you down, but you can count on the beer.

We're never going back to Prohibition, or the time not

so long ago when servers at the Ritz-Carlton ushered Betty Friedan from the bar and into the ladies' room lounge for her whiskey sour, since it just wasn't right for a woman to drink alone in public.

But maybe, just maybe, we can learn a thing or two from where we've been, and create a new approach to help women deal with a problem whose consequences in broken families, broken hearts, and broken futures, are all too real.

Acknowledgments

Sometimes when I see books on a bookshelf I think of the legions of people it takes to put them together: each one a small factory of thinkers, organizers, writers. This one is no different.

My first thanks go to Priscilla Painton, who suggested the idea of a book on women and alcohol on a wintry day when we both had colds. I sent her a proposal some weeks later, and we both thought it was a straightforward tale that would take me several months to put together. Her wisdom, keen eye, gifted pen, and infinite patience kept the book focused—and me calm. Michael Szczerban and Sydney Tanigawa are fabulous wordsmiths and technological mavens. (With such talent in ascendance, nobody should fear the End of Books.)

My agents, Glen Hartley and Lynn Chu, are tireless champions.

My reporting introduced me to women (and men) across the country who deepened my understanding of our country's relationship with alcohol, our regard for women who drink too much, and our health-care approach toward overdrinking altogether. Many thanks to the researchers and clinicians who work to employ science's answers for people who drink too much: Mary Ellen Barnes and Ed Wilson took endless hours to answer my questions, read my drafts, and hone my thinking. Dr. Mark Willenbring spoke to me many times, and read parts of the manuscript; Dr. Tim Norcross, Dee-Dee Stout, and Fred Rotgers were candid and unsparing about their experiences as treatment providers (and, in Dee-Dee's case, as a former drinker); Rick Grucza shared his research on current patterns; Sharon Wilsnack answered thousands of questions, including some I asked twice. She also described the mores surrounding women's drinking in the 1970s and helped me to understand how, despite the nation's current drinking patterns, some of those views can persist. Valerie Ramey added valuable insight on the American time deficit.

Lori Rotskoff read early chapters, and offered wisdom about the postwar climate in which A.A. flourished. Trysh Travis shared thoughts about her research into A.A.'s cultural impact, and Ron Roizen's questions improved my clarity. Madelon Powers debunked many myths.

I am grateful to all the women who spoke to me about this difficult subject, which remains, for so many, a shameful secret. Monica Richardson, Amy Lee Coy, and Jeannie Long laid bare their experiences, doubts, and battles. Ilse Thompson shared her knowledge and sharp eyes. Pamela Pecs Cytron described how sympathy seemed to come more easily to friends and neighbors when she had breast cancer than when she had been in rehab. Joy spent hours to give me an accurate picture of her life, and the program that helped her. Joanna opened up her house—and salad provisions—to me as a complete stranger, and became a friend in the process. Louise welcomed me to Ohio, offered pithy commentary, and answered legal questions throughout.

I spoke and wrote to hundreds of women whose faulty shut-off valves plague them still, and I am deeply grateful for their willingness to talk to me. Their stories help demonstrate the complexity of female drinking today, and at least some of what drives it. Samantha, a retired federal prosecutor, described how wine and vodka helped her unwind from white-knuckled days trying some of her region's most unsavory criminals. Bridget, an intelligence officer in the early days of the Iraq war, told me about the bombing deaths of the civilians for whom she felt responsible. Merlot was the only thing that helped erase the gruesome images she saw on her desk. Sharon, an engineer at one of the nation's most demanding information technology firms, told me of her failed attempts at rehab—and spoke mournfully of losing custody of her three boys because of it. Cecilia, an environmental scientist in the Gulf of Mexico, was grieving her mother's death when the Deepwater Horizon catastrophe decimated the wildlife she so cherished and had dedicated her career to protecting. There were so many others: women who patiently answered questions that were surely uncomfortable to answer—about arrests while driving drunk; about jail time; about infidelities. Many described the painful experiences of being abused at the hands of those they hoped would help them. Because so many wished to remain anonymous, their stories are woven into the background of much of what I wrote.

On my reporting trips, I had great hosts: Darieck Scott and Stephen Liacouras in San Francisco, and Michael Hawley in Los Angeles. In St. Helena, Pat Perini and Bob Long welcomed and fed me, and shared their own marvelous wines, and along with Harvey Posert and Margrit Biever Mondavi helped describe the vast changes taking place in their corner of the world in the 1970s and '80s. So, too, did Zelma Long, Axel Borg, and Ann Noble.

During the three years it took to put this together, my family was tolerant, patient, and encouraging even when I didn't reciprocate their courtesies. My daughters, Ilana, Moriah, and Dalia Engelberg, were kind, bright stars and impeccable culture-watchers, often spotting verities and memes I didn't even know existed. My sister, Michelle Glaser Jackson, listened to me talk, and helped me diagram, sometimes on place mats and used envelopes, patterns I hadn't seen myself. My sister-in-law, clinical psychologist Elizabeth Engelberg, shared her expertise about contemporary female struggles. My father-in-law, Edward Engelberg, watched out for the latest stories and studies on Americans and booze. My mother, Virginia Glaser, was a wise, kind, and thoughtful reader who gave me fabulous background on the social landscape of the 1950s, '60s, '70s, and '80s, and often challenged me to be clearer and more concise. My father, Steve Glaser, helped expand my palate—always with the moderation of which he is a model. I could not dream of better fortune than having them all in my orbit.

My neighbors and friends never told me to shut up even as I'm sure I bored them with booze talk. Thanks to Diana Arkoulakis, Martha Ann Overland, Val Thomas, Henry Reisch, Amy Putman, Nina Rosenstein, Dale Russakoff, Nomi Kehati, Netaya Anbar, Leslie Mitchel Bond, Tracy Weber, Nikole Hannah-Jones, Joyce Weatherford, Melissa Deutsch, Jennifer Dominguez, Cliff and Robin Kulwin. The great literary sage Flip Brophy listened, advised, and made soup.

I also had the great luck to marry a man who is brilliant, funny, and dazzlingly optimistic—especially when I'm not. Stephen Engelberg edited this manuscript many times, and talked me up from my book tunnel with alarming regularity. Thanks to him—for pretty much everything.

Notes

1: *Lush*

18   *In the same period, the rate for young men rose only 8 percent:* Aaron White et al, "Hospitalizations for Alcohol and Drug Overdoses in Young Adults Ages 18–24 in the United States, 1999–2008: Results from the Nationwide Inpatient Sample," *Journal of Studies on Alcohol and Drugs* 72 (September 2011): 774–86.

19   *In 2011, students at Rutgers University chose:* Gus Lubin, "State University Rutgers Paid Snooki $32,000 for a Speech about Partying and Tanning," *Business Insider* (April 4, 2011): http://articles. businessinsider.com/2011-04-04/news/29965833_1_snooki-budget -gap-commencement-address.

20   *In 2010, Gallup pollsters reported:* Gallup, "U.S. Drinking Rate Edges Up Slightly to 25-Year High" (July 30, 2010): www.gallup.

com/poll/141656/drinking-rate-edges-slightly-year-high.asp.

20 *White women are more likely to drink:* Raul Caetano et al., "Socio-demographic Predictors of Pattern and Volume of Alcohol Consumption across Hispanics, Blacks, and Whites: 10-Year Trend (1992–2002)," *Alcoholism: Clinical and Experimental Research* 34, no. 10 (October 2010). This study did not examine Asian American women, who traditionally drink less than any group in the United States due in part to their inability to tolerate alcohol. Nor did it include Native American women, whose communities have been disproportionately devastated by the toxic effects of alcohol. I also interviewed Caetano by phone on March 16, 2011.

21 *Women are the wine industry's most enthusiastic:* This figure is well known in the wine industry, and documented in many surveys and papers, including Sharon Dean et al, "Women and Wine: An Analysis of This Important Market Segment" (paper, Fifth International Wine Business Research Conference, Auckland, New Zealand, February 8–10, 2010): http://academyofwinebusiness.com/wp-content/uploads/2010/04/ForbesCohenDean-Women-and-wine.pdf.

21 *Despite the recession or perhaps because of it:* WineMarketCouncil.com, http:/winemarketcouncil.com/?page_id=35.

21 *Not all that wine is being decorously sipped:* Centers for Disease Control and Prevention, "Binge Drinking," *Vital Signs* (January 10, 2012): www.cdc.gov/vitalsigns/bingedrinking.

21 *No surprise, then, that the number of women arrested for drunk driving:* 2011 Annual Report of the California DUI Management Information System to the California Legislature: www.dmv.ca.gov/about/profile/rd/r_d_report/Section%205/S5-233.pdf.

22 *There is evidence that alcohol dependence among women:* Richard A. Grucza et al, "Secular Trends in the Lifetime Prevalence of Alcohol Dependence in the United States: A Re-evaluation," *Alcoholism: Clinical and Experimental Research* 32, no. 5 (May 2008).

22   *Sharon Wilsnack, a psychologist at the University of North Dakota:* Sharon C. Wilsnack, interview with author, March 23, 2011. Wilsnack's quotes in this chapter come from that interview and a second interview on June 14, 2011.

23   *That dovetails with what Rick Grucza, an epidemiologist:* Richard A. Grucza, interview with author, May 15, 2009.

24   *Women of childbearing age are incessantly warned that alcohol poses a danger:* For reference on this or any other physical effects, see "Women and Alcohol: What You Need to Know," Harvard Health Publications, accessed September 12, 2012, www.helpguide.org/harvard/women_alcohol.htm.

24   *In California, the number of young women responsible for alcohol-related accidents jumped: Orange County Drinking and Driving 2008 Community Forum, Executive Summary,* accessed July 2, 2010, www.ochealthinfo.com/docs/public/adept/OCHCA-Executive-summary-2009.pdf.

24   *While the number of U.S. drunk-driving deaths fell:* National Highway Traffic Safety Administration, "Traffic Safety Facts, 2010 Data," accessed September 12, 2012, www-nrd.nhtsa.dot.gov/Pubs/811606.pdf.

24   *One way to measure the changes in women's drinking habits:* Substance Abuse Treatment Admissions by Primary Substance of Abuse, Office of Applied Statistics, Substance Abuse and Mental Health Services Administration, "Treatment Episode Data Set, January 7, 2010," accessed August 12, 2012, www.samhsa.gov/data/2k10/208/208WomenAlc2k10web.pdf. The data are kept in files called the Treatment Episode Data Set, or TEDS. Of course, they reveal only the people who seek treatment, who represent a small percentage of people who actually have a drinking problem. Nevertheless, the statistics are telling.

Notes

2: We Are Women, Hear Us Pour

27   *Women are twice as likely to suffer from anxiety and depression:* Throughout my reporting, this fact was repeated frequently. See "Women and Alcohol: What You Need to Know," Harvard Health Publications, accessed September 12, 2012, www.helpguide.org/harvard/women_alcohol.htm.

28   *Until recently, nobody even thought to look at how differently alcohol:* F. Gerard Moeller, "Sex, Stress, and Drug Cues in Addiction," *American Journal of Psychiatry* (April 1, 2012): http://ajp.psychiatryonline.org/article.aspx?articleid=1090656. In this editorial, Moeller discusses several studies, including the 2012 Yale study. This is the study: Marc Potenza et al, "Neural Correlates of Stress-Induced and Cue-Induced Drug Craving: Influences of Sex and Cocaine Dependence," *American Journal of Psychiatry* (April 1, 2012): http://ajp.psychiatryonline.org/article.aspx?articleid=426881.

28   *In a study she conducted as a graduate student at Harvard:* Sharon C. Wilsnack, interview with author, March 23, 2011.

30   *Mrs. Kennedy praised their graceful simplicity:* NBC News Time Capsule: Jacqueline Kennedy: The White House Tour, February 14, 1962, accessed September 10, 2012, www.hulu.com/watch/5135. The number of viewers—56 million—was repeated frequently on the fiftieth anniversary of the tour. NPR's indomitable Sara Fishko repeated it on *On the Media,* accessed February 20, 2012, www.onthemedia.org/2012/feb/10/jacqueline-kennedys-white-house/transcript.

30   *But anybody could buy her crystal:* Jeffrey B. Snyder, "The Gavel: Morgantown Glass Graced the White House," accessed April 1, 2012, www.thegavel.net/morgan.html.

30   *When Letitia Baldrige, Mrs. Kennedy's social secretary:* Excerpt from Marie Smith, *Entertaining in the White House* (Washington,

D.C.: Acropolis Books, 1967), accessed May 10, 2012, www.jfkli-brary.org/Research/Ready-Reference/JFK-Miscellaneous-Infor-mation/Entertaining-in-the-White-House.aspx. Baldrige herself describes the reaction of the press—and teetotaling politicians—to the free-flowing liquor in a number of recollections. One is in this memoir: Letitia Baldrige, *A Lady, First: My Life in the Kennedy White House and the American Embassies of Paris and Rome* (New York: Penguin, 2002), 171–72.

31 *Rick Grucza, the Washington University epidemiologist:* Richard A. Grucza, interview with author, May 15, 2009.

31 *Between 1940 and 1960, the number of women:* Claudia Goldin et al., "The Homecoming of American College Women: The Reversal of the College Gender Gap," *Journal of Economic Perspectives* 20, no. 4 (Fall 2006): 133.

31 *By 1963, Gallup pollsters found that 63 percent:* Frank Newport et al., "Long-Term Gallup Poll Trends: A Portrait of American Public Opinion Through the Century," Gallup News Service, December 20, 1999, www.gallup.com/poll/3400/LongTerm-Gallup-Poll-Trends-Portrait-American-Public-Opinion.aspx#1.

32 *By the mid-1970s, Gallup divided respondents:* Tracey Sugar, e-mail message to author, February 15, 2012. Sugar sent me some attachments that showed the gender breakdown of the poll from 1977, 1982, and 1987. In an e-mail message to me on February 2, 2012, Sugar told me that the company doesn't have archived tabulations of polls prior to the mid-1970s.

32 *At the end of the 1970s, nearly half of all women: Women in the Labor Force, 1970–2009,* U.S. Department of Labor, Bureau of Labor Statistics chart, January 5, 2011, www.bls.gov/opub/ted/2011/ted_20110105_data.htm.

32 *Grucza calls this voyage to a new world:* Richard A. Grucza, interview with author, May 15, 2009.

33 *Harvey Posert, one of the industry's first marketers:* Harvey Posert, interview with author, February 3, 2010. Though we met three times, the recollections described here come from our second meeting, which took place on that date.

35 *A pamphlet the wine industry circulated to grocers:* This material comes from an undated pamphlet from the library of the Wine Institute in San Francisco. Posert guessed that it came from the late 1950s or early '60s.

36 *In California, where laws allowed the sale of wine in supermarkets:* Julia Flynn Siler, *The House of Mondavi: The Rise and Fall of an American Wine Dynasty* (New York: Gotham Books, 2007), 199.

37 *The University of California at Davis library has a vast collection:* UC Davis librarian Axel Borg is one of those superhuman people you feel lucky to meet. I met him for the first time on January 29, 2010, when he generously showed me the collections at the marvelous Peter Shields library. He is a giant ex-Marine with a shaved head and goatee, and an encyclopedic knowledge of California's food and wine history. The university honored him in 2011 at an awards ceremony you can read about here: http://dateline.ucdavis.edu/dl_detail.lasso?id=13748.

37 *The report, called "Wine and Women: A Ladies' Home Journal Reader Reaction":* The seventy-page report is titled simply "Wine and Women: A Ladies' Home Journal Reader Reaction Bureau Report." It lacks a date. In dozens of interviews at the University of California at Davis and in Napa and St. Helena, I met no one who could remember it.

38 *But it was clear the industry was seeking early adopters:* "Early adopters" is a phrase popularized by sociologist Everett M. Rogers in his 1962 book, *Diffusion of Innovations* (New York: Free Press, 2003). Now in its fifth printing, the book describes how new ideas disperse over time.

38 *By the early 1970s, wine was ubiquitous:* These headlines were compiled in Wine Institute Bulletins, 1970–1979. The Wine Institute Library in San Francisco kept detailed logs of wine's appearances and local news. I spotted "The Anti-Tension Diet" in *McCall's,* February 1977: 54.

38 *In the 1970s, sixty-two million newspapers were sold:* Pew Research Center's Project for Excellence in Journalism, "2004 Daily and Sunday Circulation," March 14, 2004, www.journalism.org/node/793.

39 *"Anything to get people to taste it, to familiarize themselves":* Harvey Posert, interview with author, May 18, 2010.

39 *For Margrit Biever, who would become Mondavi's second wife:* Margrit Biever Mondavi, interview with author, May 18, 2010.

40 *By the late 1970s, the quality of California wines:* At a 1976 blind tasting in Paris known as the "Judgment of Paris," a panel of judges selected a California chardonnay and a cabernet sauvignon as the top wines. The results surprised everybody.

40 *They helped put traditional little Napa on the map:* Statistics on U.S. wine consumption are from the Wine Institute, accessed June 1, 2012, www.wineinstitute.org/resources/statistics/article86.

41 *One was a young scientist named Zelma Long:* Zelma Long, interview with author, January 14, 2010.

42 *Taste tests from the early California whites:* Harvey Posert, interview with author, February 3, 2010.

42 *"For people who were new to wine, it had a rich":* Zelma Long, interview with author, September 1, 2010.

43 *depending on its alcohol content:* Vintner Bob Long, interview with author, February 2, 2010.

43 *Today, women buy nearly two-thirds of the 784 million gallons:* Andrew Adam Newman, "Marketing Wine as a Respite for Women's Many Roles," *New York Times* (August 29, 2012).

45   *Psychologist Bruce Alexander, a Canadian addiction expert:* Bruce
      K. Alexander, *The Roots of Addiction in Free Market Society*
      (Vancouver, B.C.: Canadian Center for Policy Alternatives, April
      2001), 1. In this fascinating book, Alexander points to the rise of
      addiction throughout the world—particularly when traditional
      tribal societies are crushed, or when an advanced one crumbles.

48   *A few years ago, Valerie Ramey, an economist at the University
      of California:* Valerie Ramey, interview with author, October 27,
      2010.

52   *By studying Bureau of Labor Statistics data from 1965 to 2007:*
      Garey Ramey and Valerie Ramey, "The Rug Rat Race," *Brookings
      Papers on Economic Activity* (Spring 2010): 129–76.

53   *In other words, the rise in child-care time resulted:* Ibid., 130.

54   *According to a 2009 study released by two Wharton School econ-
      omists:* Betsey Stevenson and Justin Wolfers, "The Paradox of
      Declining Female Happiness," *American Economic Journal: Eco-
      nomic Policy 2009* 1, no. 2: 190–225, August. http://bpp.wharton.
      upenn.edu/betseys/papers/Female_Happiness.pdf.

55   *"Or," Stevenson and Wolfers conclude, "women may":* Ibid., 224.

3: *I Have to See a Man about a Dog*

58   *On frigid Sunday mornings, Puritan worshipers filed:* W. J. Rora-
      baugh, *The Alcoholic Republic: An American Tradition* (New
      York: Oxford University Press, 1979), 28.

59   *"It disperseth melancholly & causeth cheerfulness":* Karen Hess,
      transcriber, *Martha Washington's Booke of Cookery and Booke of
      Sweetmeats* (New York: Columbia University Press, 1996), 397.

59   *Capon Ale:* Ibid., 393.

60   *Betsy Ross's sister was expelled:* Marla R. Miller, *Betsy Ross and the
      Making of America* (New York: Henry Holt, 2010), 247.

60 *During the Revolutionary War, General Henry Knox:* Betty Sowers Alt and Bonnie Domrose Stone, *Campfollowing: A History of the Military Wife* (New York: Praeger, 1991), 55.

60 *Rush wrote a pamphlet about the effects of alcohol:* Rorabaugh, *The Alcoholic Republic,* 39–46.

61 *In his investigation of early American drinking:* Ibid., 8.

61 *Buffalo, transformed by the completion of the Erie:* Stephen R. Powell, "Rushing the Growler: A History of Brewing and Drinking in Buffalo," accessed September 12, 2012, www.buffalonian.com /history/industry/brewing/growler/chapIII/buffsalooncapitol.html.

61 *New York State had a distillery for every:* For the number of distilleries in New York State, see Rorabaugh, *The Alcoholic Republic,* 87. For population figures, see *The State of New York Census of 1825,* New York State Library Online Catalog, accessed September 14, 2012, http://128.121.13.244:8080/awweb/main.jsp?smd =2&did=79111&nt=browse5. Census figures show a population of 1.6 million, which results in one distillery per every fourteen hundred residents.

61 *"Bread is considered the staff of life":* Kenneth L. Holmes, ed., *Covered Wagon Women: Diaries & Letters from the Western Trails,* vol. 8 (Glendale, CA: Arthur H. Clark, 1983), 252.

62 *From Tennessee to Alaska, there are nearly:* Geographical Names Information Service, U.S. Board on Geographic Names, accessed July 1, 2012, http://geonames.usgs.gov/pls/gnispublic/f?p=154:2: 4397204383716030::NO:RP::.

64 *The most popular guidance came in a magazine:* Anne C. Rose, *Voices of the Marketplace: American Thought and Culture, 1830– 1860* (Lanham, MD: Rowman & Littlefield, 2004), 75. I also found information about *Godey's* and Hale at the University of Vermont's Godey's Lady's Book website: www.uvm.edu/%7Ehag/ godey/contents.html.

64 *When she serialized T. S. Arthur's antialcohol novel:* T. S. Arthur, *Ten Nights in a Bar-Room and What I Saw There* (Bedford, MA: Applewood, 2000; originally published in Philadelphia by Lippincott, Grambo & Co., 1855). I had access to a hard copy, but I also found it on OpenLibrary.org, accessed May 2, 2012, http://archive.org/stream/10nightsinabarroom00arthrich#page/n7/mode/2up. For more, see Graham Donald Warder, "Selling Sobriety: How Temperance Reshaped Culture in Antebellum America" (Ph.D. diss., University of Massachusetts, Amherst, 2000), *Electronic Doctoral Dissertations for UMass Amherst,* Paper AAI9960803; http://scholarworks.umass.edu/dissertations/AAI9960803/.

64 *Meanwhile, a group of six ex-drinkers had formed:* The influence of the Washingtonians on the U.S. attitude toward drinking should not be underestimated. Mark Edward Lender and James Kirby Martin discuss the Washingtonians in their wonderful overview of American alcohol culture, *Drinking in America: A History* (New York: Free Press, 1987), 74–79. Daniel Okrent does as well in *Last Call: The Rise and Fall of Prohibition* (New York: Scribner, 2010), 9–12. William L. White also explores the group's history in *Slaying the Dragon: The History of Addiction Treatment and Recovery in America* (Bloomington, IL: Chestnut Health Systems, 1998), 8–14.

65 *In 1874, a group launched the Woman's Christian:* "Early History," WCTU.org, accessed May 1, 2012, www.wctu.org/earlyhistory. Hundreds of historians have written about the WTCU's influence on American society.

65 *The WCTU, which required that members be white:* Okrent, *Last Call,* gives a lively overview in chapter 1, "Thunderous Drums and Protestant Nuns." See also Andrew Sinclair, *Prohibition: The Era of Excess* (London: Faber & Faber, 2009), first published in 1962. Sinclair discusses the reformers' "textbook crusade" on pages 62 to 66. Finally, David Hanson, who blogs at *Alcohol: Problems and*

Solutions, has an excellent overview as well. He keeps a more current log of temperance leaders here: www2.potsdam.edu/hansondj/ Controversies/1124913901.html, accessed September 12, 2012.

67 *Carry Nation, a manic middle-aged Kentuckian:* I first learned about Carry Nation in Jerry Brenneman's AP history class in Albany, Oregon, and was so fascinated by her fervor, I wrote my first-ever term paper on her. I refreshed my memory with Sinclair's *Prohibition,* Okrent's *Last Call,* and of course, Nation's florid 1905 autobiography, *The Use and Need of the Life of Carry A. Nation.* You can find a digital version here: www.gutenberg.org/ dirs/etext98/crntn10.txt, accessed September 6, 2012.

68 *Over hearty chicken soup and the roar of some firefighters:* Madelon Powers, interview with author, December 4, 2010.

69 *Powers recounts the story of:* Madelon Powers, *Faces along the Bar: Lore and Order in the Workingman's Saloon, 1870–1920* (Chicago: University of Chicago Press, 1998), 210–11.

70 *Abstaining from alcohol didn't mean middle-class women:* Stephen R. Kandall, *Substance and Shadow: Women and Addiction in the United States* (Cambridge, MA: Harvard University Press, 1999), 22.

70 *They also made Lydia Pinkham a wealthy woman:* Okrent, *Last Call,* 194.

71 *Many Victorian-era women, including reformers:* Catherine Gilbert Murdock, *Domesticating Drink: Women, Men, and Alcohol in America, 1870–1940* (Baltimore: Johns Hopkins Press, 1998), 42–69.

71 *Twenty-one thousand American women had served as nurses:* "Women in the U.S. Army," www.army.mil/women/history.html.

71 *Tens of thousands more had attended college:* Claudia Goldin et al, "The Homecoming of American College Women: The Reversal of the College Gender Gap," *National Bureau of Economic Research,*

NBER Working Paper Series (March 2006): 1, http://faculty.smu. edu/millimet/classes/eco7321/papers/goldin%20et%20al.pdf.

71 *It was so common for women to join:* "Running Wild: College Students in the 1920s," accessed April 2, 2012, www.flapperjane.com/ September%2004/running_wild.htm.

72 *In* This Side of Paradise, *F. Scott Fitzgerald:* F. Scott Fitzgerald, *This Side of Paradise* (New York: Modern Library, 2001), 171.

73 *Women who, a few years before, would have blanched:* Frederick Lewis Allen, *Only Yesterday: An Informal History of the 1920s* (New York: Harper Collins, 1931), 111–12.

73 *In the first year, consumption was estimated:* Okrent, *Last Call*, p. 361.

74 *As Gilbert Murdock put it, the Eighteenth Amendment:* Gilbert Murdock, *Domesticating Drink*, p. 69.

75 *Karpman laid out his jaundiced view of female drinkers in his preface:* Benjamin Karpman, *The Alcoholic Woman: Case Studies in the Psychodynamics of Alcoholism* (Washington, D.C.: Linacre Press, 1948). These quotes, as well as the reaction to his 1934 talk, appear in the preface of the book, vii–x.

76 *He attributed the excess drinking of a patient named Frances:* Karpman dissects the poor woman in the chapter called "The Case of Mrs. Frances Elliott," Ibid., 119–223.

76 *Another patient, Vera, had a sadistic mother:* This comes from Karpman's analysis of Mrs. Vera Banchek, Ibid., 66–118.

77 *The third woman, Elizabeth, also had physically:* Karpman describes Miss Elizabeth Chesser, Ibid., 1–67.

78 *Colleagues revered Karpman, the author of dozens:* In the May 23, 1960, issue of *Time*, an unbylined article titled "Medicine: Criminal or Insane" described Karpman as "patriarchally bearded." They quoted him as saying: "Is the accused sick or not? You can't have mental illness and criminal responsibility in the same person at the same time?" When he died of a heart attack in 1962, death notices

appeared in three journals, including the *American Journal of Psychiatry*. The quoted obituary here was written by Bernard Cruvant: "Benjamin Karpman, 1886–1962." I found it here: http://ajp .psychiatryonline.org/data/Journals/AJP/2663/1119.pdf, accessed January 16, 2012. For more, take a look at Karpman's Wikipedia entry: http://en.wikipedia.org/wiki/Benjamin_Karpman.

78   *A New York columnist described the "Bistro Berthas":* These snippets from the news appear in an excellent chapter in the anthology *Altering American Consciousness: The History of Alcohol and Drug Abuse in the United States, 1800–2000* (Amherst and Boston: University of Massachusetts Press, 2004). The chapter "Lady Tipplers: Gendering the Modern Alcoholism Paradigm, 1933–1960" was written by Michelle McClellan, an assistant professor of history at the University of Michigan.

79   *Noel Busch, a writer at* Life *magazine:* Noel F. Bush, "Lady Tipplers: Suggestions Are Offered for Improving Their Behavior," *Life* (April 14, 1947), 85. I found a paper copy that belonged to a collector friend, but you can see the piece for yourself here. It is a stunning reminder of how casually sexist U.S. society was: http://books. google.com/books?id=ik0EAAAAMBAJ&printsec=frontcover&-source=gbs_ge_summary_r&cad=0#v=onepage&q&f=false.

79   *It went through several printings in the 1950s:* This information comes from Amazon.com, accessed April 7, 2012, www.amazon. com/The-Alcoholic-Woman-Benjamin-Karpman/dp/B000RT-FUBS/ref=tmm_mmp_title_0.

4: One Day at a Time: A.A. and Women

81   *Founded by two men in the mid-1930s:* Many sources, on and off the record, referred openly to A.A.'s rocky early history with women; Marty Mann, the first woman who is said to have become

sober in A.A., discussed it at Alcoholics Anonymous meeting in Toronto, July 1965. A recording is available at http://cpaulus. com/talks/OldTimers/MartyMann.mp3, accessed September 14, 2012. William L. White describes it in *Slaying the Dragon*, 158–62.

For this chapter, I consulted many Wilson biographies and films, as well as his own writings. They include *Alcoholics Anonymous,* Fourth Edition (New York: Alcoholics Anonymous World Services, 2001); *As Bill Sees It* (New York: Alcoholics Anonymous World Services, 1967); Wilson's own *Alcoholics Anonymous Comes of Age* (New York: Alcoholics Anonymous World Services, 1957); and *Not-God: A History of Alcoholics Anonymous,* by Ernest Kurtz (Center City, MN: Hazelden, 1979). I also relied on these biographies: Francis Hartigan, *Bill W.: A Biography of Alcoholics Anonymous Cofounder Bill Wilson* (New York: Thomas Dunne Books, 2000); Susan Cheever, *My Name Is Bill: His Life and the Creation of Alcoholics Anonymous* (New York: Washington Square Press, 2004); and Nan Robertson, *Getting Better: Inside Alcoholics Anonymous* (New York: William Morrow, 1988).

Cheever has written about her own experiences with A.A., and is on the board of the National Council on Alcoholism and Drug Dependency, originally founded by Marty Mann. Hartigan served as Lois Wilson's personal secretary. Robertson, who died in 2009, was a journalist at the *New York Times* for four decades. I met her when I worked there as a news assistant the year she retired.

There is a great deal more less flattering information about Wilson on blogs that are critical of A.A., but even these biographies, from within the A.A. community, reveal untrustworthy traits in a man who encouraged others to be "rigorously honest."

82 *In more than 90 percent of the nation's rehab facilities:* Mark Willenbring, M.D., interview with author, May 13, 2011. Willenbring is a psychiatrist in private practice in the Twin Cities, and from

2004 to 2009 served as director of the Treatment and Recovery Research Division of the National Institute on Alcohol Abuse and Alcoholism/National Institutes of Health.

83 *Patients called the method, which had been developed:* Cheever, *My Name Is Bill*, 13.

84 *Like many innovators, Wilson was complicated:* Hartigan describes Wilson's paranormal and LSD experiments in *Bill W.*, pages 176 to 179, and describes his womanizing at length on pages 190 to 197. Robertson touches on his womanizing in *Getting Better*, pages 36, 40, and 84.

85 *As the group spread, Wilson and other early members:* The twelve steps of Alcoholics Anonymous are listed in Alcoholics Anonymous World Services, *Alcoholics Anonymous*, 59–60. The title of the chapter is "How It Works." The steps remain unchanged since the first edition.

THE TWELVE STEPS OF ALCOHOLICS ANONYMOUS

1. We admitted we were powerless over alcohol—that our lives had become unmanageable.
2. Came to believe that a Power greater than ourselves could restore us to sanity.
3. Made a decision to turn our will and our lives over to the care of God *as we understood Him.*
4. Made a searching and fearless moral inventory of ourselves.
5. Admitted to God, to ourselves, and to another human being the exact nature of our wrongs.
6. Were entirely ready to have God remove all these defects of character.
7. Humbly asked Him to remove our shortcomings.
8. Made a list of all persons we had harmed, and became willing to make amends to them all.

9. Made direct amends to such people wherever possible, except when to do so would injure them or others.

10. Continued to take personal inventory and when we were wrong promptly admitted it.

11. Sought through prayer and meditation to improve our conscious contact with God, *as we understood Him,* praying only for knowledge of His will for us and the power to carry that out.

12. Having had a spiritual awakening as the result of these Steps, we tried to carry this message to alcoholics, and to practice these principles in all our affairs.

86 *But in the A.A. worldview, a woman's most:* Alcoholics Anonymous World Services, *Alcoholics Anonymous,* chapter 5, "To Wives," 111. This chapter remains in the most recent edition. A.A.'s website maintains that Bill Wilson wrote the chapter against his wife Lois's wishes. Accessed February 15, 2012, www.aa.org/subpage.cfm?page=287#tres.

86 *"To my lot falls the rather doubtful distinction":* Florence R., "A Feminine Victory." This story appeared in the first edition of *Alcoholics Anonymous,* but later was omitted after she died, having returned to drinking. Her story can be found at http://fellowship12.com/index.php?option=com_content&view=article&id=110&Itemid=172, accessed September 13, 2012. Her biography appears on www.silkworth.net, "A New Light: The First Forty," accessed September 13, 2012, http://silkworth.net/dickb/thefirstforty.html.

86 *Records from the period show the men of A.A. worried:* Anonymous, "The Good Old Times," *Grapevine* 42, no. 1 (June 1985).

87 *But few men tolerated alcoholic women:* Sally Brown and David R. Brown, *A Biography of Mrs. Marty Mann: The First Lady of Alcoholics Anonymous* (Center City, MN: Hazelden, 2001), 116.

87 *To manage this potential distraction:* White, *Slaying the Dragon,* 158.

87 *Women-only meetings developed, too:* Ibid., 160.

87 *Her name was Marty Mann, and in 1939:* Brown and Brown, *A Biography,* gives a deeply researched and unvarnished view of Mann's life.

88 *To the men, Mann recalled, she was:* Marty Mann, Toronto speech, 1965.

89 *"This was a man's problem and A.A. was":* Ibid.

89 *As late as 1959, Mann noted disapprovingly:* Marty Mann, in a 1960 pamphlet called "For Men Only? AA Today: A Special Publication by the AA Grapevine Commemorating the 25th Anniversary of Alcoholics Anonymous" (New York: AA Grapevine, The International Journal of Alcoholics Anonymous, 1960): 33, www. barefootsworld.net/aaformenonlygvjune1960.html.

89 *"We hide," she said. "We do our drinking":* Mann, Toronto speech, 1965.

90 *Science could boost the movement, and so the research:* Ron Roizen, "The American Discovery of Alcoholism, 1933–1939" (Ph.D. diss., University of California, Berkeley, 1991), accessed September 14, 2012, www.roizen.com/ron/disshome.htm. Roizen's dissertation has been exceedingly helpful to me in this research, as has Roizen, who is a lively and generous conversationalist and even more energetic e-mailer. Roizen discusses the connection between brewers and early alcoholism studies on his blog, www.roizen. com/ron/sidetracked.htm.

90 *Mann attended the Yale summer school:* Ron Roizen delves into this here: www.roizen.com/ron/rr11.htm, accessed September 14, 2012. He explains it this way: Roizen queried University of Leipzig's archivist, K. Gaukel, about Jellinek's degrees. Gaukel found Jellinek's records as a linguistics and history student—but never a degree of any kind, and certainly not a medical one. I also checked with Stanford University, where Jellinek was working

when he died of a heart attack in 1963, for confirmation of what Jellinek had claimed on his résumé before being hired. Drew Bourn, curator at the Stanford Medical History Center, Lane Medical Library & Knowledge Management Center, told me in an e-mail (May 13, 2011) that Jellinek's file listed the following institutions: University of Berlin 1908–1910; University of Grenoble, France, 1910–1911; University of Leipzig 1911–1914; M.Ed., 1913; Sc.D., 1936. Roizen dug up other interesting jobs, including stints at a hospital in Hungary for "nervous children"; as a currency trader; at a steamship line in Sierra Leone; and as a banana researcher for United Fruit in Honduras—all before turning to alcohol research. Like Roizen, I think that somebody ought to do a biography of the guy. Whatever you want to say, he had a fascinating life.

91 *Data for one of his early studies:* Trysh Travis, "Points: The Blog of the Alcohol and Drugs History Society: What Time Do You Want It to Be, Part Two, May 28, 2011," http://pointsadhsblog. wordpress.com/2011/05/28/what-time-do-you-want-it-to-be-part-two.

91 *This left ninety-eight self-selected white men:* E. M. Jellinek, "Phases in the Drinking History of Alcoholics: Analysis of a Survey Conducted by the Official Organ of Alcoholics Anonymous," *Quarterly Journal of Studies on Alcohol* (June 7, 1946): 1–88. You can also see a reprint of the 1946 paper here, including a footnote in which Jellinek explains why he tossed the female responses: http://silkworth.net/sociology/Soc04OCR.pdf.

91 *Over the next many years:* You can see a copy of an early rendering of the chart here: http://pointsadhsblog.wordpress.com/2011/05/28 /what-time-do-you-want-it-to-be-part-two.

Historians caution about the need to view documents and attitudes in the context of the period, but by the early 1940s researchers had developed penicillin and sulfa drugs; antihistamines;

and vaccines that offered protection from typhus, yellow fever, and pertussis. So judging by those standards, it's hard to believe this was ever considered science.

British alcohol researcher Max Glatt published a study in which he concluded that group therapy was useful for alcoholics. It built on Jellenek's earlier work and chart, this time using a parabola. M. M. Glatt, "Group Therapy in Alcoholism," *The British Journal of Addiction,* vol. LIX, No. 2, January 1958.

92 *The misapplication of the word could only undermine:* E. M. Jellinek, "Phases of Alcohol Addiction," *Quarterly Journal of Studies on Alcohol* (December 13, 1952): 673–84.

92 *He acknowledged that his conclusions were:* E. M. Jellinek, *The Disease Concept of Alcoholism* (Mansfield, CT: Martino Publishing, 2010), 38.

92 *At a 1959 alcoholism conference at Columbia University:* Arthur H. Cain, "Alcoholics Anonymous: Cult or Cure?" *Harper's* (February 1963), 48. Cain was a psychologist who admired A.A. in its early days, but grew dismayed when it began to grow "ritualistic." He traced its popularity to a slew of positive magazine and newspaper stories in the 1940s.

93 *Jellinek wrote that "recovered alcoholics in Alcoholics Anonymous speak of":* Jellinek, *The Disease Concept of Alcoholism,* 41.

93 *In his book* Alcohol: The World's Favorite Drug: Griffith Edwards, *Alcohol: The World's Favorite Drug* (New York: Thomas Dunne, 2000), 97.

94 *Marty Mann was remarkably gifted at spinning the bottle:* Marty Mann is a revered figure in the twelve-step community, and she certainly had a lot of guts. The Brown and Brown biography, *A Biography of Mrs. Marty Mann,* gives a reverential but clear-eyed view of her personal life. Ron Roizen draws a more complete picture, rounding out her professional aims (and compromises) in

his blog: http://www.roizen.com/ron/mann.htm, accessed June 26, 2013. He points out some rather startling details about her massaging of facts in what endures, at least culturally, in our concept of alcoholism. I also read Mann's own books: *Marty Mann Answers Your Questions about Drinking and Alcoholism* (New York: Holt, Rinehart and Winston, 1970) and *Marty Mann's New Primer on Alcoholism: How People Drink, How to Recognize Alcoholics and What to Do about Them* (New York: Holt, Rinehart and Winston, 1958). That title alone is a bold assertion about just how alcoholics could be *fixed*. Mine is a 1981 edition.

94   *In the 1940s, newspapers and national magazines:* There were many stories that sparked interest in the group, but perhaps the most important was written by Jack Alexander in the popular weekly *The Saturday Evening Post,* on March 1, 1941. His piece, "Alcoholics Anonymous: Freed Slaves of Drink, Now They Free Others," generated thousands of letters to A.A.'s office in New York. Eight years after publication, Bill Wilson wrote to Alexander to request a follow-up that would give an "inside view" of the organization. Alexander complied, and wrote a second piece, "The Drunkard's Best Friend," that ran in the *Post* on April 1, 1950. The correspondence is available on A.A.'s website: www.aa.org/lang/en/subpage.cfm?page=472, accessed September 19, 2012.

94   *On radio and television shows, men poured out:* You can find a list of the appearances here: http://silkworth.net/aagrowth/mich_Detroit.html. Detroit media magnate William Edmund Scripps was an admirer of the group, and helped to publicize it in his outlets.

94   *In 1945, moviegoers turned* The Lost Weekend: As I was researching this chapter, for a couple of weeks my kids would come home from school and find me watching old movies. My youngest daughter was about eight or nine when she tiptoed into my room for a pencil, and whispered to a playmate that Mom was "working

even if she didn't look like it." It hardly felt like it. *Some Like It Hot* (released 1959) is funny enough to "disperseth melancholly," and Richard Burton and Elizabeth Taylor soar in *Who's Afraid of Virginia Woolf?* ("Martha, rubbing alcohol for you?" "Sure. Never mix, never worry!" (released 1966). As a kid, I watched the *Thin Man* movies with my grandmother, who was a big fan of Myrna Loy. I was too young to really get the cocktail jokes, but it was so much fun to be with my giggling grandmother, I laughed alongside her. I watched parts of some of the films again, and was amazed at how stark the contrast was between the first *Thin Man* movie, in 1934, and *The Lost Weekend,* eleven years later. I'm hardly the first person to notice this, of course: Cultural historian Lori Rotskoff examines these films, along with gender and society, in her wonderfully titled *Love on the Rocks: Men, Women, and Alcohol in Post-World War II America* (Chapel Hill: University of North Carolina Press, 2002).

It is obvious but important to note that films in midcentury America were immensely influential. Long before our splintered universe of cable and the Web and tweets, we had movies, and their messages had impact. The *Thin Man* pictures debuted in 1934, the year after the repeal of Prohibition and in the midst of the Depression. The film *The Lost Weekend* appeared after a protracted, frightening war.

It's one tough slog of a movie, but it at least acquainted me with the work of Charles Jackson, author of the novel on which the film is based. Jackson became a star in A.A.—as long as he was sober. He was a frequent speaker at meetings throughout the 1950s, opening up to crowds about his hubris, hobnobbing with Judy Garland and Frank Sinatra, as well as his use of the barbiturate Seconal. (You can hear a 1959 speech he gave in Cleveland at www.xa-speakers.org/pafiledb.php?action=file&id=1797, accessed September 19, 2012.) He left the program for good, though, in the early '60s, and died alone in a Chelsea hotel room in 1968, OD'd on sleeping pills. For more on this sad history, see the rere-lease of Jackson's short story collection, *The Sunnier Side: Arcadian Tales,* with an introduction by John W. Crowley (Syracuse, NY: Syracuse University Press, 1996).

95   *Director Blake Edwards later said he had quit drinking:* Steve Garbarino, "The Silver Panther Strikes Again," the *New York Times* (August 19, 2001).

96   *"Women Drunkards, Pitiful Creatures, Get Helping Hand":* Box 459, News and Notes From the General Service Office of A.A, "Welcome to Your General Service Office," vol. 49, 29, no. 2 (April–May 2003), accessed May 1, 2012, www.aa.org/en_pdfs/en_box459_april-may03.pdf.

96   *In 1946, the* Grapevine, *the group's monthly:* Grace O., "Women in AA Face Special Problems," *Grapevine,* 3, no. 5 (October 1946).

97   *A.A.'s most prominent initiative for women was Al-Anon:* Hartigan, *Bill W.,* 71. Eric Pace, "Lois Burnham Wilson, a Founder of Al-Anon Groups, Is Dead at 97," *New York Times* (October 6, 1988).

97   *Cultural historian Lori Rotskoff suggests:* Rotskoff, in *Love on the Rocks,* examines the role of A.A. in shaping marital politics in an especially lively and original chapter called "The Dilemma of the Alcoholic Marriage." The social worker's quote is found on page 154.

98   *Speaking to a Canadian audience celebrating:* Mann, Toronto speech, 1965.

5: *Rehab Nation*

99   *In 1970, the United States formally embraced:* NIH Almanac, accessed April 20, 2012, www.nih.gov/about/almanac/organization/NIAAA.htm.

99   *After addressing alcoholism, Congress declared war on cancer:* Office of Government and Congressional Relations website, National Cancer Institute, National Cancer Act of 1971, accessed April 20, 2012, http://legislative.cancer.gov/history/phsa/1971.

100   *In the years that followed, Mann's group:* NCADD.org, accessed April 20, 2012, www.ncadd.org/history/decade4.html.

100   *Government funding accounted for more:* Charles Bufe, *Alcoholics Anonymous: Cult or Cure?* (Tucson: Sharp Press, 1998), 110.

100   *At the same time, major insurers recognized alcoholism:* The government had come to accept alcoholism as an illness. Two federal appeals courts had dismissed charges of public inebriation against two men on the grounds that they were sick, and that conviction would be in violation of the Eighth Amendment, which prohibits the federal government from imposing cruel and unusual punishment. See more by Albert B. Logan, "May a Man Be Punished Because He Is Ill?" *American Bar Association Journal* 52, no. 10 (October 1966): 932–37. Also see Bufe, *A.A.: Cult or Cure?,* chapter 8, "A.A.'s Influence on Society," 105–28, accessed September 13, 2012, http://home.earthlink.net/~bbaa.library/AA_Cult_or_Cure.pdf.

101   *The counselors established a group:* Nancy Olson, *With a Lot of Help from Our Friends: The Politics of Alcoholism* (Lincoln, NE: Writers Club Press, 2003), 24–25.

101   *Consider this: In 1969, the outgoing Johnson administration:* Ibid., 72.

101   *In 1972, the NIAAA budget was:* Ibid., 192–96.

101   *In 1973, there were roughly 1,800 treatment:* National Admissions to Substance Abuse Treatment Services: The Treatment Episode Data Set (TEDS) 1992–1995, accessed March 12, 2012, www.samhsa.gov/data/DASIS/teds00/teds_rpt_2000_web.pdf, 6.

101   *By 2009, that number had jumped to more:* "2009 State Profile— United States National Survey of Substance Abuse Treatment

Services," accessed March 12, 2012, wwwdasis.samhsa.gov/webt/
state_data/US09.pdf.

101 *In 2012, the NIAAA's budget was $469 million:* National Institute
of Alcohol Abuse and Alcoholism, accessed September 19, 2012,
www.niaaa.nih.gov/about-niaaa/our-funding/congressional-bud-
get-justification/fy-2012-congressional-budget.

101 *Government-supported researchers have discovered:* Bruce Booth,
"Cancer Drug Targets: The March of the Lemmings," Forbes.
com, accessed June 20, 2012, www.forbes.com/sites/brucebooth
/2012/06/07/cancer-drug-targets-the-march-of-the-lemmings.

101 *Yet there are about a mere six drugs:* The emetic effects of disulfiram were discovered by accident in the 1940s, when Danish researchers drank alcohol while testing the drug on themselves for
its ability to fight parasites. It was approved by the Food and Drug
Administration in 1951. Naltrexone was approved by the FDA in
1994. You can read more about disulfiram in this paper by Helge
Kragh, "From Disulfiram to Antabuse: The Discovery of a Drug,"
Bulletin for the History of Chemicals 33, no. 2 (2008), accessed
September 20, 2012, www.scs.illinois.edu/~mainzv/HIST/bulle-
tin_open_access/v33-2/v33-2%20p82-88.pdf .

102 *As more Americans entered rehab:* Trysh Travis, *The Language of
the Heart: A Cultural History of the Recovery Movement, from
Alcoholics Anonymous to Oprah Winfrey* (Chapel Hill: University
of North Carolina Press, 2009), 274.

102 *By 1968, females accounted for:* White, *Slaying the Dragon,* 161.

102 *Sociologists found that married American women:* Arlie Hochschild, *The Second Shift* (New York: Avon, 1989), 3.

102 *In national drinking surveys taken in 1967:* David J. Pittman and He-
lene Raskin White, eds., *Society, Culture, and Drinking Patterns Re-
examined* (New Brunswick, NJ: Alcohol Research Documentation,
Inc., Rutgers University, 1991), table 2, 164. I found this in chapter

5, "Changes in American Drinking Patterns and Problems, 1967–1984," by Michael E. Hilton and Walter B. Clark. The chapter was reprinted from the *Journal of Studies on Alcohol* 48 (1987), 515–22.

102 *And in that seventeen-year gap:* Pittman and White, *Society, Culture, and Drinking,* table 3, 166.

103 *There were other dramatic social changes:* National Center for Health Statistics, *Monthly Vital Statistics Report* 39, no. 12, supplement 2 (May 21, 1991).

103 *Though American women had begun to drink:* Marcia Russell, Maria Testa, and Sharon Wilsnack et al, "Alcohol Use and Abuse," in *Women & Health* (San Diego: Academic Press, 2000), 589–98. The book was edited by Marlene B. Goldman and Maureen C. Hatch.

103 *The discovery in the 1970s and '80s:* Elizabeth M. Armstrong and Ernest L. Abel, "Fetal Alcohol Syndrome: The Origins of a Moral Panic," *Alcohol and Alcoholism* 35, no. 3 (2000): 276–82.

104 *Mustering her courage, Wilsnack asked her professor:* Sharon C. Wilsnack, interview with author, March 23, 2011.

105 *Not far from Wilsnack's office, the authors of:* Information about *Our Bodies, Ourselves* comes from the authors' terrific website, accessed May 1, 2012, www.ourbodiesourselves.org/about/jamwa.asp.

106 *By 1976, the increasingly significant NIAAA:* Olson, *With a Lot of Help,* 306.

106 *"No single national data source covers":* Leigh Henderson, epidemiologist at the Substance Abuse and Mental Health Services Administration, e-mail message to author, June 16, 2011.

106 *In sociological surveys designed to test tolerance:* Florence Ridlon, *A Fallen Angel: The Status of the Female Alcoholic* (Cranbury, NJ: Associated University Presses, 1988), 25.

107 *In 1976, the Rand Corporation released results:* David J. Armor et al, *Alcoholism and Treatment* (Santa Monica, CA: Rand Corp., 1976). The introduction was enough to set off a firestorm (see pag-

es v to vii). But read the whole thing, which people are still arguing about, even though it's science: accessed May 29, 2010, www.rand. org/content/dam/rand/pubs/reports/2007/R1739.pdf.

107 *Separately, two California researchers, Mark and Linda:* Stanton Peele, "Through a Glass Darkly," *Psychology Today* (April 1983): 38–42, www.peele.net/lib/glass.php.

108 *Prominent NCA board members tried to suppress:* Lender and Martin, *Drinking in America,* 201.

108 *In response to the criticism, Rand researchers:* J. Michael Polich et al, *The Course of Alcoholism: Four Years after Treatment* (Santa Monica, CA: Rand Corp., 1980), accessed May 29, 2010, www. rand.org/content/dam/rand/pubs/reports/2006/R2433.pdf.

108 *They were accused of fraud:* M. B. Sobell et al, "Alcohol Treatment Outcome Evaluation Methodology: State of the Art 1980–1984," *Addictive Behaviours* 12 (1987): 113–28.

108 *The root of the angry responses was obvious:* Alan G. Marlatt, interview with author, October 12, 2009.

109 *For proponents of twelve-step programs:* A.A. World Services, *Alcoholics Anonymous,* 31.

109 *At about the same time, another academic:* Biographical information on Jean Kirkpatrick comes from Jean Kirkpatrick, *Goodbye Hangovers, Hello Life* (New York: Atheneum, 1968), chapter 1. The quote is found on page xv.

110 *But what really rankled her was the notion:* Ibid., 111–69.

111 *Betty Ford left the White House:* Enid Nemy, "Betty Ford, Former First Lady, Dies at 93," *New York Times,* July 8, 2011, www. nytimes.com/2011/07/09/us/politics/betty-ford-dies.html?pagewanted=all.

111 *Elizabeth Taylor and Liza Minnelli told their:* Gioia Dillberto, "Stars in Rehab: Breaking the Cycle," *People,* August 6, 1984, www.people.com/people/archive/article/0,,20088392,00.html.

111 *Drew Barrymore checked in as a teenager:* "Rehabbed Stars: How Betty Ford Helped," accessed July 13, 2011, www.people.com/people/gallery/0,,20509577_20986930,00.html.

111 *Elsewhere, Ann Richards campaigned for governor:* Maura Casey, "Ann R., Alcoholic," *New York Times,* September 16, 2006, www.nytimes.com/2006/09/16/opinion/16sat4.html.

111 *Between 1968 and 1989, the number of women:* White, *Slaying the Dragon,* 161.

111 *In 1990, Ms. magazine published:* Charlotte Kasl, "The Twelve-Step Controversy," *Ms.,* November/December 1990, 30–31.

112 *In the early days of A.A., Bill Wilson:* A.A. World Services, *Alcoholics Anonymous,* xvi.

112 *Results are released to researchers sporadically:* Don McIntire, "How Well Does A.A. Work? An Analysis of Published A.A. Surveys (1968–1996) and Related Analyses/Comments," *Alcoholism Treatment Quarterly* (December 2000), 1–18.

113 *Actor Charlie Sheen even mentioned it:* Jeannine Stein and Mary Forgione, "Charlie Sheen Claims A.A. Has a 5% Success Rate—Is He Right?" *Los Angeles Times,* March 3, 2011, http://articles.latimes.com/2011/mar/03/news/la-heb-sheen-aa-20110302.

113 *"The problem with the conclusions drawn":* Don McIntire, "How Well Does A.A.Work?," 5.

113 *She identified herself as Carol McIntire:* Carol McIntire, interview with author, July 7, 2011.

113 *"He kept his work to himself":* Carol McIntire, interview with author, July 7, 2011.

114 *A.A.'s most recent member survey:* Alcoholics Anonymous, 2011 Membership Survey, accessed September 24, 2012, www.aa.org/pdf/products/p-48_membershipsurvey.pdf.

114 *In it, they wrote:* Arthur S., Tom E., and Glenn C., "Alcoholics Anonymous Recovery Outcome Rates: Contemporary Myth and

Misinterpretation," January 1, 2008, accessed July 12, 2011, http://hindsfoot.org/recout01.pdf.

115   *The first time I went, the place felt like Lourdes:* I visited the GSO building several times in 2010. The first scene I describe took place on May 7, 2010.

116   *On the second visit, I was with:* This meeting and the quotes come from the interview with Joy. on June 11, 2010.

117   *In part because of this, Trysh Travis:* Travis, *The Language of the Heart*, 11.

117   *"Many people revere the idea of experience":* Trysh Travis, interview with author, March 21, 2012.

118   *At the end of her life, Elizabeth Taylor was:* Brooks Barnes, "Gay Bar Mourns Elizabeth Taylor," *New York Times*, March 24, 2011.

118   *"It's like trying to study the 'effectiveness' of yoga":* Mark Willenbring, interview with author, May 13, 2011.

119   *A comprehensive analysis in the* Cochrane Review: M. Ferri et. al, "Alcoholics Anonymous and Other 12-Step Programmes for Alcohol Dependence," *Cochrane Database System Review* (July 2006). I have a hard copy, but the abstract is available here: www.ncbi.nlm.nih.gov/pubmed/16856072. Not everyone was pleased with the report. In an August 2008 letter to the editor of the journal *Addiction*, Lee Ann Kaskutas, a senior scientist at the Alcohol Research Group in Emeryville, California, called the Cochrane report "misleading," accessed September 24, 2012, http://onlinelibrary.wiley.com/doi/10.1111/j.1360-0443.2008.02240.x/full.

119   *Psychologist and author Stanton Peele noted:* Stanton Peele, interview with author, September 7, 2011.

119   *Alan Marlatt called it "poorly conceived":* Bruce Bower, "Alcoholics Synonymous: Heavy Drinkers of All Stripes May Get Comparable Help from a Variety of Therapies," *Science News*, January 25, 1997, http://lifering.org/1997/08/alcoholics-synonymous-heavy-

drinkers-of-all-stripes-may-get-comparable-help-from-a-variety-of-therapies.

119 *In a reanalysis of the data published:* Robert Cutler and David Fishbain, "Are Alcoholism Treatments Effective? The Project MATCH data," *BMC Public Health* (July 2005), www.biomed-central.com/1471-2458/5/75.

119 *And, as Willenbring pointed out, the studies were largely:* Mark Willenbring, interview with author, September 22, 2011.

120 *As more and more women entered twelve-step programs:* Cheever, *My Name Is Bill*, 231.

A note: As I began my research on this sexual predation in A.A. in 2010, I consulted many Wilson biographies, and spoke to a number of "old-timers." I drew my own conclusions, but in 2012, while reading the *Orange Papers*, an online analysis of A.A., I noticed that Orange, the site's curator, had cited many of the same details. You can read them here: www.orange-papers.org/orange-otherwomen.html#ftnt03, accessed March 15, 2012. The site is amazingly comprehensive. In a January 19, 2011, e-mail, Orange, as he is called, told me that he gets about a million hits a month.

6: *The Thirteenth Step*

121 *For years, Monica Richardson, a singer and actress:* I first spoke to Richardson by phone in the winter of 2011. February 2010 began a vivid e-mail and phone correspondence, and we met in person in July 2012. Her notes of her time in A.A. are extensive, and she read many versions of this chapter for accuracy.

121 *"We are like men who have lost their legs":* A.A. World Services, *Alcoholics Anonymous*, 30.

123 *A.A. discourages sexual relationships between longtime members:* A.A World Services, *Alcoholics Anonymous: Twelve Steps & Twelve*

Traditions (New York: Alcoholics Anonymous World Services, 1952), 119, accessed May 1, 2012, www.aa.org/twelveandtwelve/en_copyright.cfm. It suggests that members get together romantically only when they are "solid" A.A.s who have known each other long enough to know that their "compatibility at spiritual, emotional and mental levels is a fact and not wishful thinking."

126 *Some researchers have found that women:* Sharon C. Wilsnack et al, "Childhood Sexual Abuse and Women's Substance Abuse: National Survey Findings," *Journal of Studies on Alcohol and Drugs* (May 1997): 264–71. This research has been replicated many times, and Wilsnack, in several telephone conversations, reiterated its importance.

126 *Psychologist Charlotte Davis Kasl writes that:* Charlotte Davis Kasl, *Many Roads, One Journey: Moving beyond the 12 Steps* (New York: Harper, 1992), discusses this phenomenon in detail in chapter 10, "Boundaries and Sexual Exploitation, or Why Do I Have This Knot in My Gut?," which begins on page 230.

126 *Since the group's first days in Akron:* A.A. pamphlet, *Questions and Answers on Sponsorship*, 9, accessed May 2, 2012, www.aa.org/pdf/products/p-15_Q&AonSpon.pdf. Also in A.A. World Services, *Alcoholics Anonymous Twelve & Twelve*, 119.

127 *A 2010 sociology journal found that:* Jolene M. Sanders, "Acknowledging Gender in Women-Only Meetings of Alcoholics Anonymous," *Journal of Groups in Addiction & Recovery* 5, no. 1 (2010), 17–33. I did a random search on A.A. websites for women-only meetings in northern New Jersey, the greater Boston area, Atlanta, and metropolitan Seattle. Of the thousands of meetings listed in each area, roughly 6 percent were women-only.

127 *Four percent said they had been raped by:* Cathy J. Bogart, "'13th-Stepping': Why Alcoholics Anonymous Is Not Always a Safe Place for Women," *Journal of Addictions Nursing: A Journal for the Prevention and Management of Addictions* 14, no. 1 (2003):

Notes

43–47. I also spoke with Bogart by phone on November 28, 2011. She told me that she had submitted the study to several journals, but that it was only accepted by one. "Everybody acknowledges this exists," she told me that day, "but few people want to face it."

128 *I also read the creepy diary of Sean:* Brandon Hanson, "Sex Offender Sent to Jail for Preying on Women in A.A.," *Lake County Leader Advertiser,* April 6, 2012, http://leaderadvertiser.com/news/article_201455de-7e9f-11e1-9514-0019bb2963f4.html.

128 *This, too, fits a pattern, and manipulators:* Kasl, *Many Roads, One Journey,* 233–34.

129 *When she first joined A.A., Gwen said:* "Sexual and Financial Predators in A.A., Parts 1 and 2," *Safe Recovery,* Richardson's Internet radio show, Blogtalkradio.com, episodes 41 and 43, May 10, 2011, and May 24, 2011. On these shows, the two women recalled their first meeting in 2009. I use a pseudonym to protect Gwen's identity, but she used her real name on these shows.

130 *She found several blogs that were critical:* Richardson saw the *Orange Papers* (www.orange-papers.org) for the first time, as well as two articles: Marc Fisher, "Midtown Group: AA Group Leads Members Away from Traditions," *Washington Post,* July 22, 2007, www.washingtonpost.com/wp-dyn/content/article/2007/07/21/AR2007072101356_pf.html; and Nick Summers, "A Struggle Inside A.A," *Newsweek,* May 6, 2007, www.thedailybeast.com/newsweek/2007/05/06/a-struggle-inside-aa.html.

For additional information on this story, I spoke with Fisher on November 8, 2011. We also exchanged e-mails that day.

131 *"I pimped [them] out":* Fisher, "Midtown Group."

131 *While A.A. instructs members not to "play doctor":* Pamphlet, *The AA Member—Medications and Other Drugs* (New York: A.A. World Services, Inc., 2011), accessed May 7, 2012, www.aa.org/pdf/products/p-11_aamembersMedDrug.pdf.

132 *I asked A.A.'s General Service Office:* I met Mary C., the public information officer at A.A. in person for an interview on July 13, 2010, but I asked this question by e-mail on December 10, 2011. I received a response on December 20, 2011.

132 *When ex-Midtown members contacted:* Fisher, "Midtown Group," and Summers, "A Struggle Inside A.A."

133 *It warned that "the organization has the potential to become":* Gerard Seenan "Drink Advice Service Confronts Sex Abuse," *The Guardian,* July 4, 2000, www.guardian.co.uk/uk/2000/jul/05/gerardseenan?INTCMP=SRCH.

133 *In the leaked documents, A.A. nonalcoholic trustee:* Letter by Alcoholics Anonymous General Service Board trustee, "Reason for Topic and Additional Background Information: Predators in A.A.," July 29, 2007. You can see it on the *Orange Papers,* accessed September 22, 2011, www.orange-papers.org/ATTACHMENT_TO_TOPIC_002-PREDATORS.pdf. In communications with the trustee, who verified the document, I agreed to maintain his anonymity.

134 *The British behavioral guidelines include:* "Personal Conduct Matters," *Guidelines for A.A. in Great Britain,* no. 17 (April 2002): 63–65.

134 *Written against the backdrop of the* Washington Post*:* A.A. trustee, "Reason for Topic and Additional Background."

135 *It was written by a woman whose:* Letter to *Grapevine,* July 1993.

136 *In October 2009, more than two years:* General Service Board, Subcommittee on Vulnerable Members in A.A., *Final Subcommittee Report* (October 27, 2009). Also in the *Orange Papers,* accessed September 22, 2011, www.orange-papers.org/ATTACHMENT_TO_TOPIC_002-PREDATORS.pdf.

137 *Here's the key passage:* General Service Board, *Final Subcommittee Report.*

137   *The Alcoholics Anonymous groups oppose no one:* The Big Book Online, Appendices, www.aa.org/bigbookonline/en_appendicei. cfm, accessed January 15, 2013.

140   *Richardson was stunned when:* Mary Vorsino, "Murder-Suicide Leaves 3 Dead," *Honolulu Star-Advertiser,* August 21, 2010, www .saradvertiser.com/news/20100821_Murder-Suicide_leaves_3_dead. html?id=101217004. Rob Perez, "Red Flags Missed," *Honolulu Star-Advertiser,* November 7, 2010, www.staradvertiser.com/ news/20101107_Red_flags_missed.html?id=106. Brooks Baehr, "Combat Stress and Rejected Marriage Proposal May Have Triggered Rage," August 21, 2010, www.hawaiinewsnow.com/global/ story.asp?s=13024225.

141   *The former trustee:* Former trustee, interview with author, December 6, 2011.

141   *But some of his friends did:* Marc Fisher, e-mail, November 8, 2011.

141   *Ellen Dye, a Washington-area psychologist:* Ellen Dye, Ph.D., interview with author, October 4, 2011.

142   *"Who's going to believe a drunk girl":* Amy Lee Coy, interview with author, July 16, 2011.

142   *She likens it to the Penn State sex abuse:* Louise, e-mail, September 26, 2012.

142   *In a forum on the anti-A.A. blog:* "A.A. and 13th-Step Victims," June 13, 2011, post on www.orange-papers.org/forum/node/150.

142   *"What was 'my part'":* Safe Recovery Online Radio, May 24, 2011, www.blogtalkradio.com/saferecovery.

143   *"Thirteenth stepping is a big problem":* Comment made to me during my tour of the General Service Office, June 11, 2010.

144   *The Boy Scouts, for instance, issued guidelines:* "Open Letter to Our Parents," accessed September 26, 2012, www.scouting.org/ sitecore/content/BSAYouthProtection/BSA_Communications/ parent_letter.aspx.

144   *Victor Vieth, a former Minnesota prosecutor:* Victor Vieth, interview with author, April 26, 2012.

144   *As Mary C. . . . wrote:* Mary C., e-mail, December 20, 2011.

144   *In April 2012, Richardson posted an accounting:* "Leaving A.A.," accessed April 24, 2012, http://leavingaa.com/?p=858#comment-4223.

7: *Twenty-First-Century Treatment*

147   *Joanna made two big decisions when she turned fifty:* Joanna's narrative comes from repeated interviews in person, by e-mail, and on the phone, with Joanna herself, though that is not her real name. All other details are correct, but because she lives in a small Pennsylvania town where she and her husband are business owners, she prefers to maintain her privacy. I met her through Ed Wilson and Mary Ellen Barnes, who approached her about telling her story. She readily agreed, and I met her for the first time at her home on July 14, 2010. The quotes and narrative attributed to her come from that interview and ones that followed over the next two years. Like Monica Richardson, Joanna, Mark Willenbring, Ed Wilson, and Mary Ellen Barnes read and vetted everything written about them.

150   *Immediately Joanna liked what she read:* Like Joanna, I found Barnes and Wilson by typing the same thing into Google: www.non12step .com. I met them for the first time at their office on May 19, 2010.

151   *Addictions counseling licensing requirements:* Basic Level Certification, NAADAC, Association for Addiction Professionals, accessed June 10, 2011, www.naadac.org/certification/535.

153   *The morning of their first meeting:* Dr. Tim Norcross, interview with author, August 4, 2011.

153   *If the client is in good health:* National Center for Biotechnology Information Bookshelf, "Oral Naltrexone at a Glance," accessed August 11, 2011, www.ncbi.nlm.nih.gov/books/NBK64042.

154　*In 2006, the NIAAA released the results:* Raymond F. Anton et al., "Combined Pharmacotherapies and Behavioral Interventions for Alcohol Dependence/The COMBINE Study: A Randomized Controlled Trial," *Journal of the American Medical Association* 295, no. 17 (May 2006): 2003–17, http://jama.jamanetwork.com/article.aspx?articleid=202789.

155　*The FDA approved acamprosate, used extensively:* "FDA Approves New Drug for Treatment of Alcoholism: FDA Talk Paper," July 29, 2004, http://web.archive.org/web/20080117175319/http://www.fda.gov/bbs/topics/answers/2004/ANS01302.html.

155　*Topiramate, an anticonvulsant:* Bankole Johnson et al., "Topiramate for Treating Alcohol Dependence," *Journal of the American Medical Association* 298, no. 14 (October 7, 2007): 1641–651, http://jama.ama-assn.org/content/298/14/1641.full.

155　*Meta-analyses have shown that oral:* There have been many. Here is a recent one: S. Rosner et al., "Opioid Antagonists for Alcohol Dependence," *Cochrane Library* 12 (2010), accessed September 27, 2012, www.thecochranelibrary.com/details/file/884765/CD001867.html.

155　*In a study of the use of extended-release naltrexone:* S. S. O'Malley and P. G. O'Connor, "Medications for Unhealthy Alcohol Use: Across the Spectrum," *Journal of the National Institute on Alcohol Abuse and Alcoholism* 33, no. 4 (2011), accessed September 24, 2012, http://pubs.niaaa.nih.gov/publications/arh334/300-312.htm.

155　*But some small studies have reported that naltrexone:* B. E. Setiawan et al., "The Effect of Naltrexone on Alcohol's Stimulant Properties and Self-Administration Behavior in Social Drinkers: Influence of Gender and Genotype," *Alcoholism: Clinical and Experimental Research Journal* 35, no. 6 (June 2011): 1134–41. You can see the abstract here: www.ncbi.nlm.nih.gov/pubmed/21410481, accessed

June 10, 2012. A team of Spanish researchers found optimistic signs for the gene marker as well: A. J. Chamorro et al., "Association of μ-Opioid Receptor (OPRM1) Gene Polymorphism with Response to Naltrexone in Alcohol Dependence: A Systematic Review and Meta-Analysis," *Addiction Biology* 17, no. 3 (May 2012): 505–12, www.ncbi.nlm.nih.gov/pubmed/22515274.

156 *Another study showed promising signs for naltrexone's:* Jennifer Tidey et al, "Moderators of Naltrexone's Effects on Drinking, Urge and Alcohol Effects in Non-Treatment Seeking Heavy Drinkers in the Natural Environment," *Alcoholism: Clinical and Experimental Research Journal* 32, no. 1 (January 2008): 58–66, www.ncbi.nlm. nih.gov/pmc/articles/PMC2743136. This study found the drug reduced drinking days among those with a gene called DRD4-L, but did not moderate effects for those with the OPRM1 gene. This was a small study, however, and I include it because of the drug's notable effects on women.

157 *In Finland, however, an American doctor:* John David Sinclair, "Evidence about the Use of Naltrexone and for Different Ways of Using It in the Treatment of Alcoholism," *Alcohol and Alcoholism* 36, no. 1 (2001): 2–10. You can also find an explanation of Sinclair's methods at his website: http://thecureforalcoholism.com, accessed September 27, 2012.

157 *But he says it helps to prepare a problem drinker:* Ed Wilson, interview with author, October 26, 2010.

157 *Joanna wasn't looking for magic, though:* Again, this narrative comes from repeated interviews with Joanna, Mary Ellen Barnes, and Ed Wilson in 2011, as well as an interview with Tim Norcross, to whom I spoke on August 4, 2011.

158 *Wilson administers one designed in the 1970s:* Jane Loevinger, ed., *Technical Foundations for Measuring Ego Development* (Mahwah, NJ: Erlbaum, 1998), 53. Susanne R. Cook-Greuter further devel-

oped Loevinger's stage theory. For more information, see www. stillpointintegral.com/docs/cook-greuter.pdf, accessed September 27, 2012. For a brief background on Loevinger, see "Women's Intellectual Contributions to the Study of Mind and Society," accessed October 26, 2010, www.webster.edu/~woolflm/loevinger. html.

163   *Like Joanna, Wilson's and Barnes's clients:* These numbers come from Ed Wilson, interview with author, September 21, 2011. He and Barnes follow up with their clients by phone and e-mail regularly.

165   *Often, they are also dedicated exercisers:* M. T. French et al, "Do Alcohol Consumers Exercise More? Findings from a National Survey," *American Journal of Health Promotion* 24, no. 1 (September–October 2009): 2–10, http://ajhpcontents.org/doi/abs/10.4278/ajhp.0801104.

167   *Tim Norcross, the family doctor who treats:* Tim Norcross, interview with author, August 4, 2011.

168   *Mark Willenbring, psychiatrist and former director:* Mark Willenbring, interview with author, May 13, 2011. His website is http://mattsub.blogspot.com/2011/02/alltyr-is-born.html.

168   *In 2011, Stout cofounded AA2.org:* Dee-Dee Stout, interview with author, February 24, 2011. Stout's book *Coming to Harm Reduction Kicking and Screaming: Looking for Harm Reduction in a 12-Step World* (Bloomington, IN: Author House, 2009) offers a new look at the different modes of recovery from alcohol and drug abuse. You can learn more about her group at www.aa2.org.

169   *Ken Anderson, a community organizer in Brooklyn:* Ken Anderson, interview with author, January 10, 2012.

169   *Stanton Peele, a New Jersey psychologist:* Stanton Peele, interview with author, September 7, 2011.

169   *Consider the case of Audrey Kishline:* The tragedy of Audrey Kishline inspires continued debate. I first learned of her in an

NBC Dateline episode called "Road to Recovery" that aired September 1, 2006. For a transcript see www.msnbc.msn.com/id/14627442/ns/dateline_nbc/t/road-recovery/, accessed September 21, 2011. You can also see some of the online debate about her, including Peele's comment, on Dr. Alexander DeLuca's website, "Addiction, Pain, and Public Health Website," www.doctordeluca.com/Documents/KishlineToldMM.htm, accessed September 21, 2011.

170 *Willenbring looks forward to the day when Americans:* Mark Willenbring, interview with author, September 22, 2011.

170 *In fact, the number of Americans:* Mark Olfson and Steven C. Marcus, "National Patterns in Antidepressant Medication Treatment," *Archives of General Psychiatry* 66, no. 8 (August 2009), http://archpsyc.jamanetwork.com/article.aspx?articleid=483159.

170 *Of those patients, more than half:* Nancy Shute, "Antidepressant Use Grows, As Primary Care Doctors Do the Prescribing," "Shots," Health News from National Public Radio, August 4, 2011, www.npr.org/blogs/health/2011/08/06/138987152/antidepressant-use-climbs-as-primary-care-doctors-do-the-prescribing.

170 *By contrast, Willenbring says, fewer than 10 percent:* Mark Willenbring, interview with author, September 22, 2011.

172 *From Sweden to Australia, Denmark to South Africa:* International Center for Alcohol Policies, "International Drinking Guidelines," accessed June 6, 2012, www.icap.org/PolicyIssues/DrinkingGuidelines. ICAP is a nonprofit organization in Washington, D.C., that is funded by a number of large alcohol producers.

172 *Women in those countries live the longest:* European Commission, *Mortality and Life Expectancy Statistics,* accessed October 24, 2012, http://epp.eurostat.ec.europa.eu/statistics_explained/index.php/Mortality_and_life_expectancy_statistics.

172 *On the Greek island of Ikaria:* Dan Buettner, "The Island Where People Forget to Die," *New York Times Magazine,* October 24, 2012, www.nytimes.com/2012/10/28/magazine/the-island-where-people-forget-to-die.html?src=me&ref=general.

173 *American women, meanwhile, die sooner:* Sabrina Tavernese, "Life Span Shrinks for Less-Educated Whites in the U.S.," the *New York Times,* September 20, 2012, www.nytimes.com/2012/09/21/us/life-expectancy-for-less-educated-whites-in-us-is-shrinking.html?pagewanted=all.

173 *According to Dr. Raul Caetano:* Raul Caetano, interview with author, March 16, 2011.

174 *Fred Rotgers, a New Jersey clinical psychologist:* Fred Rotgers, interview with author, December 11, 2011.

174 *According to the Pew Research Center:* Pew Forum on Religious and Public Life, "Faith on the Hill: The Religious Composition of the 113th Congress," analysis, accessed January 12, 2013, http://www.pewforum.org/government/faith-on-the-hill--the-religious-composition-of-the-113th-congress.aspx#new. Of the 533 members, 128 were evangelical Christians whose denominations forbid alcohol, including Baptists, Methodists, Holiness, Adventist, and Congregationalist; 15 were Mormon; 2 were Muslim.

175 *Yet a 2011 study of 106,000 women in the* Journal of the American Medical Association: Wendy Y. Chen et al., "Moderate Alcohol Consumption during Adult Life, Drinking Patterns, and Breast Cancer Risk," *Journal of the American Medical Association* 306, no. 17 (November 2, 2011): 1884–890.

175 *But Dr. Steven A. Narod:* Steven A. Narod, "Alcohol and Risk of Breast Cancer," editorial, *Journal of the American Medical Association* 306, no. 17 (November. 2, 2011), 1920–1921. http://jama.jamanetwork.com/article.aspx?articleid=1104569.

176 *Dr. Lisa Schwartz, a professor of community:* Quotes are from

Dr. Lisa Schwartz, interview with author, December 19, 2011. Schwartz's editorial, "Promoting Healthy Skepticism in the News: Helping Journalists Get it Right," appeared in *Journal of the National Cancer Institute* 101, no. 23 (November 20, 2009): 1596–99. She wrote it with Steve Woloshin and Barnett S. Kramer.

Conclusion

181 *They've provided a growth market for:* Annabel Jackson, "Why Women Drink Wine: A Survey by Vinexpo Exposes the Gender Politics behind a Glass of Vino in Asia," June 25, 2010, www.cnn-go.com/hong-kong/women-and-wine-asia-430659. For information in India, see Pavos Kakaviatos, "Indian Women Drive Surge in Wine Consumption," November 7, 2011, www.decanter.com/news/wine-news/529492/indian-women-drive-surge-in-wine-consumption.

181 *Indeed, in Uganda, the number of young:* Sharon C. Wilsnack, interview with author, March 30, 2012. Wilsnack studies women and alcohol around the globe.

181 *Advertisers have taken note:* Video, Serengeti Beer, accessed March 30, 2012, www.youtube.com/watch?v=0zU5s6t29tA.

181 *We're never going back to Prohibition:* Gail Collins describes this story in *When Everything Changed: The Amazing Journey of American Women from 1960 to the Present* (New York: Little, Brown, 2009), 24.

Permissions

1. © North Wind Picture Archives.

2. © Michael J. Deas.

3. © North Wind Picture Archives.

10. Reprinted with permission from the National Council on Alcoholism and Drug Dependence, Inc. (NCADD) www.ncadd.org.

   About NCADD: The National Council on Alcoholism and Drug Dependence, Inc. (NCADD) and its Affiliate Network is a voluntary health organization dedicated to fighting the Nation's #1 health problem—alcoholism, drug addiction and the devastating consequences of alcohol and other drugs on individuals, families and communities.

Index

records destroyed by, 153
study of patients in, 107–9,
    119–20
twelve-step programs in, 82,
    100
women in, 24–25
religion:
    A.A. as faith-based, 25, 82–
        84, 88, 90, 123
    and alcoholism, 94
    and Congress, 174
    and immigration, 65–66
    "let go and let God," 97
    and morality lessons, 63–67
    and sex scandals, 133, 134,
        143, 144
    and wine, 33
religious revivals, 63
Remick, Lee, 95
Revere, Paul, 59
Richards, Ann, 111
Richardson, Dorothy, 69
Richardson, Monica, 121–45
    and A.A. double standard,
        123–24
    as A.A. member, 122–23, 127,
        145
    and A.A. refusal to act, 136–
        40, 143
    adolescence of, 121–22
    childhood sexual abuse of,
        125–26
    commitment to A.A., 128–
        29, 132, 140, 145
    Internet radio show of, 142
    and Ken, 122–24
    leaving A.A., 145

and Mr. X, 133, 134–36,
    138–39
researching thirteenth step,
    130–35
as service representative,
    128–29, 140
singing career of, 125, 133
and *Stop13stepinaa.com,* 139
in therapy, 125–26
trying to stop the abuse,
    134–39, 140, 143–45
Ride, Sally, 43, 44
risk, living with, 178
Rock, Chris, 145
Roe v. Wade, 102
Rorabaugh, W. J., 61
Rosado, Leandra, 12
Ross, Betsy, 60
Rotgers, Fred, 174
Roth, Lillian, 95
Rotskoff, Lori, 97
rum:
    in colonial times, 57, 58, 59,
        60
    "Demon Rum," 68
Rush, Benjamin, 60, 84
Rutgers University, 19

saloons, 58, 61, 68–70, 79
Schuler, Diane, 11
Schwartz, Lisa, 176–77
Sears, Roebuck, 70
Second Great Awakening, 63
Secular Organizations for
    Sobriety (SOS), 145, 168
self-awareness, 159
sensory science, 41

About the Author

Gabrielle Glaser is the author of *The Nose: A Profile of Sex, Beauty, and Survival* and *Strangers to the Tribe: Portraits of Interfaith Marriage*. She is an award-winning journalist whose work on the intersection of health and culture has appeared in the *New York Times*, the *New York Times Magazine*, the *Economist*, and many other publications. She lives with her family in Montclair, New Jersey.